YOU CAN'T LEAVE ME NOW

THREE STORIES OF TRUE CRIME

YOU CAN'T LEAVE ME NOW

THREE STORIES OF TRUE CRIME

LAURA MCNEAL

SAN DIEGO
Reader
SAN DIEGO READER BOOKS
SAN DIEGO, CA

You Can't Leave Me Now: Three Stories of True Crime
ISBN 978-1-939938-04-6

The Death of Judy Huscher
The Last Meeting of the Dove Club: A Pioneer Family's Tragedy
The Toothpicks: A Mexican Cartel in San Diego

LAURA MCNEAL
Copyright © 2014 Laura McNeal, All Rights Reserved
Versions of each story originally appeared in the San Diego Reader
and are also available as individual eBook editions:

The Death of Judy Huscher
The Last Meeting of the Dove Club: A Pioneer Family's Tragedy
The Toothpicks: A Mexican Cartel in San Diego

Published by SAN DIEGO READER BOOKS
WWW.SDREADERBOOKS.COM

San Diego *Reader*
2323 Broadway
San Diego, California 92102 U.S.A.

Design by Jessica Wentzel
Cover Photo by David Phillipich
Publishing Services by Sellbox.com

CONTENTS

FOR JUDY AND CARROLL

PREFACE

The three stories in this volume are about real crimes. The names are the names of real people. The things that happened to them, and the things they did to others, were recounted in great detail in criminal trials under oath, and all of that detail was written down by court reporters. Autopsies, trial transcripts, gravestones, closed-circuit surveillance cameras, and police reports provided the facts.

In the three crimes at the center of these stories, there's a common element beyond geography: family ties become a cage for the victim, a motive for the murderer, and a curse for the next of kin. In "The Death of Judy Huscher," a 12-year-old girl is given hot chocolate by her mother and found dead the next morning. In "The Last Meeting of the Dove Club" a son must report the murder committed by his father. In "The Toothpicks," a man drives alone to a deserted drive-in movie theater with a ransom for a kidnapper who has threatened to send his cousin home in pieces, and who in turn claims to be avenging the death of his murdered brother.

In all of these crimes, the killer acts out of an aggrieved sense of loneliness and betrayal, as if to say, in the most violent way possible, "You can't leave me." In each family, though, there is also at least one person who betrayed no one, showed courage and loyalty, and stayed true to the end.

THE DEATH OF

JUDY HUSCHER

MORNING

he body lies in a position of repose, a 12-year-old girl in pajamas, on her bed, in Fallbrook, California. Her blue eyes, though open, see nothing, and for ten more minutes, no one sees her. No one knows yet that the sheets and Judy's pajama top are stained with chocolate, that her neck is stained with chocolate, that a section of yellow toilet paper on the bed beside her is stained with chocolate, or that her arms are folded across her chest and will not be, cannot be, unfolded again. No one knows that a spoon lies balanced on her lips.

In the kitchen, the Sunday-morning light has long fallen on a saucepan, a coffee cup still puddled with brown liquid, a jar of Sanka, and an empty brown bottle of strychnine, from which the label has been peeled. No one has eaten breakfast here or read the paper or turned on the radio to hear the weather forecast for March 31, 1957. There's an empty carton of chocolate ice cream in the trashcan. In the dining room, four pill bottles and a handwritten note rest on the table, high above the head of the woman stretched out on the floor, snoring through the morning she had meant not to see.

> Dean,
> I told you last October I was too weary and then to get the terrific shock after I had tried so hard. Well, maybe this is

what you wanted??
Best to you,
Gladys
Please thank Johnsons and Rileys.

Then, as an afterthought, in shaky red pencil, nearly illegible:

If you had stayed away as you desired I think
I could have come out of it.
You tantalized me.

A horse stands at some distance from the house, waiting for tires on the driveway, the sound of footsteps, the approach of hay. It's 10:30. Judy's father, Carroll Dean Huscher, is already in his car, driving slowly through downtown Fallbrook, population 3000, the shops closed and silent, his daughter's horse waiting to be fed, his daughter's body undiscovered, the clouds dissolving like footprints in the sky above Knoll Park Lane.

TALK

Around town, they'll say she was given strychnine in an ice cream cone. They'll say Gladys told Judy that if she went to bed early, she could have ice cream, pudding, hot chocolate, or a milkshake. They'll say that Mrs. Huscher (Mrs. *Husher*, as they'll unconsciously revise her name) spent quite a bit of time stuffing toilet paper into Judy's mouth to keep her screams from arousing the neighbors. They'll say it's a black spot on the town.

They'll not believe Gladys did it — not the home ec teacher, not the Girls' League advisor, not the woman who taught you to set the table and make white sauce. Some, including her family, will say Carroll drove her to it. Some will say she was out of her mind with love for him, and when he left her, she came unhinged. Some will say he beat her, that he beat Judy, that if Gladys killed Judy she did it to protect Judy from him. Darker still, that he molested Judy. "Maybe he abused her, or maybe he was going to abandon them both," said a man who knew Judy from church and school. "He could get rid of both his problems. People were saying how it didn't take him long to get a new girlfriend."

Children will come to their own conclusions. "The children who knew Judy," said a woman who was 11 when Judy died. "What were we supposed to do? Knowing that she was dead, and, we were told — absolutely — killed by her own mother. How do you file information like that? Under what?"

"Judy wasn't gorgeous or brilliant," said a man who was in Judy's sixth-grade class. "She was just as smart as the rest of us, but her mother was really educated, and [Judy] wasn't good enough for her."

Some will have nightmares, some will forget about it, and some will talk about it in the new high school home ec room, the one Gladys was busy moving into that exhausting, unbearable spring. Some will stay in Fallbrook, and some will move to other states, countries, continents. They will grow up and have troubles that make them wonder what really happened 45 years ago and what they have just imagined.

"As we repeat a story to ourselves, in our own mind, some flaw in the accuracy of that story becomes embedded as part of the 'memory,'" said another classmate. "Most of us trust our own memories."

The memories they trust are part fiction, part fact.

"I will tell you what I know, based on what my older sister and mother told me way back then," said still another classmate. "Mr. Huscher got his divorce. I wouldn't know if he had played around or had good reason to get out of his marriage. But a few years later, he was remarried and wanted his daughter to live with him and his new wife. He prevailed in court and was awarded custody. In the night (or final weekend) Mrs. Huscher retaliated by cooking up a good mug of delicious hot chocolate and served her daughter some laced with strychnine. She herself took only enough sleeping pills to conk herself out. When they found her later, she was sleeping peacefully and very much alive. But Judy had died. What a coward this lady was…fast asleep while her daughter suffered."

As they go on forgetting and remembering, moving away, staying on, Carroll Dean Huscher will live for 31 more years. He'll store Judy's things in a box — 25 figurines of animals, a vase the size of a thimble, a Mickey Mouse bowl that says "Hello Judy," a postcard of a deer. In the basement of the San Diego Courthouse, someone will file a tight dark spool of film containing documents from the trial. Transcripts, reports, certificates, and forms will be entombed in the library, the sheriff's archives, the coroner's office, the Bureau of Vital Statistics.

In Fallbrook, the memories of all three of them, false or true, bitter or fond, will move like the Mexican ghost La Llorona, the woman who, having killed her own children, haunts the streets, crying as if to remind you that the worst thing of all can happen, the thing you could not before imagine.

DEAN

Judy called him Daddy and his wife called him Dean, but to everyone else he was Carroll. He was small, thin, and bowlegged, partial to bow ties and cowboy boots, though not at the same time. He wasn't a handsome man, really, but his glasses, his high forehead, his pointed nose, and his close-cut oiled hair made him look congenial and spruce, especially when he was clapping his hands together at the end of a good joke.

On that Sunday morning in 1957, 49-year-old Carroll Huscher was a successful man.

"A signal honor was bestowed on Fallbrook's popular Carroll D. Huscher last week," announced the *Fallbrook Enterprise*, "when he was elected President of the National Frozen Food Locker Institute at a huge meeting of members attending the industry's annual National Convention at Hotel Morrison, Chicago."

Food had always been his livelihood. At 10, he delivered it, at 24, he helped his father sell it, and at 31, he preserved it at Huscher's Froz-N Foods, which he later called "C" Huscher's Meats. There you could freeze the deer you shot, the pig you raised, the side of beef you intended to eat all winter. You rented a drawer, large or small, and after Mr. Huscher cut and wrapped the various parts, into the drawer they went, all ready for you to pick up once a week on your way through town. He sold regular cuts of meat, too, and frozen vegetables.

"Mr. Huscher liked kids," remembered a woman who shopped there as a child. "When I'd want to go into the locker with Mother, or any other child wanted to go in with his or her parent, Mr. Huscher would be buttoning up fronts, rolling up sleeves, and wrapping up little ones right along with the parent. All the jackets were for adults, so much rolling, wrapping, and buttoning was necessary (and then we probably looked pretty bizarre!). If you didn't go into the locker but waited out in the main room and Mr. Huscher wasn't busy, he'd chat with you, something most adults aren't comfortable doing."

Mr. Huscher kept his name on the meat locker even after he left the daily operation in 1955 to open a strawberry-freezing co-op a block away.

"My sister and a lot of her age group worked evenings at the strawberry plant processing berries for freezing," said a graduate of '55. "They washed, sorted, picked rot (the worst job), and put them in freezer containers," which were five-gallon gold tins with lots of sugar on top.

"I remember him opening the strawberry packing plant — it meant lots of jobs for people in Fallbrook," said the son of a high school teacher.

Carroll and Gladys had been married for 23 years, but by 1957 they weren't living together. Gladys and Judy lived in the house on Knoll Park Lane, and Carroll lived in the strawberry plant. The reasons for this were about to become public knowledge.

He started his car on Sunday morning, March 31, and set out to see Judy and feed her horse. The weather was mild and encouraging, the cool, bright spring that came every year with its orange blossoms and roses and pink India hawthorn hedges. Fallbrook lay in the hills 60 miles north of San Diego, 15 miles east of the sea, where the sun made almost every day feel like a fresh start, gleaming with possibility.

In downtown Fallbrook, the shops were closed and silent, the windows full of stuffed rabbits and Easter eggs, the sorts of things

Judy would like. On Valentine's Day, the last holiday that had involved gifts of chocolate, Mr. Huscher had driven through town with two Valentines, one for Gladys and one for Judy, because this had seemed like the best course, but it wasn't. Gladys refused hers, and then Judy said to her mother, "Why are you so mean to my daddy?"

He turned left onto Knoll Park Lane, a street of respectable teachers and plumbers and shopkeepers, of arrival and modest prosperity. The grass in the yards was bright green. He knew the neighbors up and down the street: Leighton Harrison of the drugstore, his boys Eddie and Kermit, Bill Toomey of the high school, the Reeds, Ogdens, Aabergs, and Earls. He wasn't really one of them anymore, now that he'd moved out, but his daughter's horse was waiting to be fed, and Judy was waiting too, in his mind, because he'd told her he was coming when she called to say good night.

The newspapers were still at the curb, though. Two fat Sunday papers, the *Union* and the *Times*. That startled him because Judy loved to read the funnies on Sundays.

Judy had seemed fine the day before. When Gladys picked Judy up from the strawberry co-op at 4:30, Gladys had complained about how many hours it took her to buy supplies for the home ec students — "as many hours on a Saturday, when she wasn't paid to work, as on weekdays, when she was."

He parked the car and turned off the ignition. It was 10:35 a.m. No one came out, and no one appeared at the living room window when he shut the car door. He walked behind the house to lead the horse up for water, passing, as usual, the window of his former bedroom and Judy's window, where the blinds weren't open. There was a gap of four inches, he noticed. He walked on and fetched the horse, then led him to the trough. There's nothing to do while a horse drinks, so he walked back to the front of the silent house. That's when he noticed the shades were down in Gladys's room too. The shades were down, and the light was on.

"Something about it startled me," he told police, "so I came around and took the horse back and tied him up real quick and came and looked in the window, here, the youngster's."

At Judy's window, he cupped his hands around his face. Everything changed then, past, present, and future.

"I shaded my eyes from the sun and I seen that her lips were blue."

He'd worked at an undertaker's before, and he knew how a body looks. Her bed was so close to the window that he could see the strange color of her lips, the teaspoon that was balanced across her mouth. Why a spoon? How did it get there? He reached in his pocket and found a 50-cent piece. He tapped hard on the window, to attract her attention, but she didn't move. She didn't move at all.

He had a key to the house, of course, so he went to the service porch and unlocked the back door. He shoved it open, but the chain was on. He went back to the yard to find a stick, then used it to push the chain up and down, trying to free the knob from the slot. It didn't work, so he slit the screen, reached in, and slid out the chain.

It was then that he saw his wife.

"I saw Mrs. Huscher. She was lying on the floor with her head towards the kitchen door, and her feet towards the hall door going into the bedroom, and she was snoring." Snoring in spite of how close she was to the door he'd just rattled and poked and pushed open.

"She was on her side. I turned her over on her stomach, removed her glasses and tried artificial respiration, and I got nowhere. I ran into the bedroom to see how the child was. I was sure she was gone. I found her in the condition you see her in, cold and stiff, rigor mortis had set in, and a spoon was laying across her mouth, and I picked up the spoon and as I picked up the spoon, I realized that I had picked up something that wasn't right, and I dropped it, and there was also, it looked like a piece of Kleenex, or a roll of toilet paper, and I didn't know whether it looked like it had been a gag or not, but it had the appearance to me that it could have been used for such, and I came out here and then into the dining room, and I called Dr. Powell and he was out here within three or four minutes, and he took over."

Dr. Powell had been in Fallbrook since 1941. He delivered babies and saw older patients too, such as Gladys, for whom he had prescribed the pills that were collected on the dining room table.

Dr. Powell told Mr. Huscher that his wife was in bad shape and that his daughter had been dead a number of hours. He assured Carroll there was nothing he could have done for Judy. He said it was too bad, though, that Judy hadn't lain on her side when she was vomiting. "Maybe she could have gotten rid of some of it," he said.

"Up to then," Carroll told the police, "he didn't know anything about this damn strychnine, and that stuff, so I don't know, I'm just relating the conversation."

Dr. Powell called an ambulance to take Gladys to the hospital, and one of the Harrison boys came out to watch. He wasn't the only one to notice the police cars, of course, the going in and coming out. In a town where the constable's usual job was to grab Carlin Yokum by the ear and make him roll the stop sign back to its place on the corner of Main and Alvarado (Carlin and his friends were always hiding the sign behind Westfall's in hopes there'd be a crash), somebody was bound to tell somebody why there were cops at the Huscher place on Sunday.

It was one o'clock when Deputy Bob Majors, head of what was called the Crimes of Violence Division, walked into the house. He wore a dark suit, a white shirt, a tie, and a hat. His steel-rimmed glasses were round and official-looking, like the hat. He was there to detect things.

Judy was still in her bedroom, but Gladys was gone. A sergeant was taking photographs of Judy, the kitchen sink, and the ice cream carton in the trash. Another sergeant was dusting for fingerprints. Carroll Huscher had been in the house with his daughter's body for two and a half hours when Deputy Majors and the coroner sat him down for the first interrogation.

"Would you state your full name, Mr. Huscher?" Majors asked.

Carroll stated it, but the deputy wrote it down wrong. "*Harold B. Huscher,*" Majors wrote.

"And your age?"

"Forty-nine."

And so on, through the address, Judy's full name, his wife's full name, all the easy questions.

"And now, about how long have you been estranged from your wife, or separated and not living here?" asked the deputy.

"Better than 90 days," Carroll said.

"And during that time, the daughter has been living with her. Now, as I understand it, yesterday you had the daughter with you for part of the day. Is that right?"

"From a quarter of one," Huscher said, "to approximately 4:30 in the afternoon."

"Did you come here to the house and get her?"

"Her mother brought her to me and came and picked her up."

"Is that a usual circumstance?"

"That is the usual circumstance. Either I come here and get her or she will bring her to me."

In those days, Fallbrook was a small town with the usual small-town attractions. The air-conditioned Mission Theater was three short blocks away from Huscher's business, and on the weekend of Judy's death, the main feature was *Oklahoma!* The soda fountain was two blocks away, as was Reader's store. Sometimes, at the far end of Main Street, a company like a traveling circus would lay down a wooden floor, set up a canvas tent, and let you skate all day for 25 cents. A lady played the organ, and when she stopped, you stopped.

"It was the kind of town where you could walk up Main Street and not get hit by a car," said a woman who was 16 in 1957. "We never locked our doors, never locked our cars, everybody knew everybody else. You could walk to the Mission Theater and back after a movie in the dark without being afraid."

"Now briefly," asked Deputy Majors, "what is the reason that you and your wife are separated?"

"Well, briefly," Carroll said, "is that I apparently couldn't satisfy her in any shape, way, or form, just a condition that piled up over a number of years, and I felt that if I would move out of the house — I asked in about last October. I thought it would be best, and she said that she would prefer that I would stay here but come and go as I please, if that was agreeable."

But it wasn't agreeable.

"About Christmastime or shortly before, she said she felt that maybe I was right, and she was wrong, and possibly that I should leave the premises and stay elsewhere, that I would have the right of visitation and have the child and come here and take care of matters, which I have done daily. The daughter has a horse and I have fed it each morning and each evening. I picked up the laundry, and once or twice a week I brought the cleaning woman here, each day of the week, and brought her here and picked her up and taken her back. Our relation has been very amicable, we agreed upon a property settlement between us, it was all arranged so far, and she seemed to be agreeable to it. She's a teacher in high school and people come in to visit her on that score, but I think it was just a case of too much career in the family."

Carroll Huscher found a nearly neutral truth in that moment: it was not his wife's fault or his own fault but the fault of all the work they had to do. His implication, however, was that his wife's work tipped the scales. He would state this as the problem over and over again in the days to come, and so would Gladys. The work made her weary. It came between her and Carroll, between her and Judy.

Sitting in his altered house for those two and a half hours, next to the empty bottles of pills, the strange note, the strychnine bottles, remembering what Gladys had said to him and he to her, he fixed upon an issue that was still latent in Fallbrook in 1957: women's work.

"Now, briefly, what is the reason that you and your wife are separated?"

Carroll Huscher was a private man. He didn't gossip, and he didn't talk about his personal life with men at the Rotary. When he drove a babysitter to his house and back, he didn't ask questions about how she liked school, what her plans were for the summer. He was quiet. He just drove.

When a man wearing a badge and holding a pencil asked him why he and his wife separated, Carroll Huscher kept two important details to himself. He never mentioned that he was having an affair, and he never mentioned what might have been considered motive for that affair: his banishment to the living room sofa. Perhaps he hoped these two unflattering facts wouldn't need to be known.

"Were you planning on getting a divorce?" the deputy asked.

"Well, Mrs. Huscher had gone to see her lawyer," Carroll said, "and then I'd talked it over with her, and she told me what she had had to say," and Carroll went down around the first of March and had the papers drawn up. With the lawyer, Charles Provence, they'd agreed upon joint custody of Judy. "We seemed to have an understanding," he told the deputy. "If we lived in the same town, I was to have her six months out of the year, and if we didn't, why, she would have her during the school year, and I would have her at all vacation times."

They talked a little about the attorney, about Carroll's occupation, about where he was living, at 129 E. Hawthorne Street, the same address as the strawberry plant.

"Now, do you live there alone," asked the deputy, "or do you live with somebody else?"

"I live alone."

"Have you ever been arrested?"

"No, sir, other than for traffic."

"Now, has your wife been doctoring any?"

"Yeah, she had a, she had a tumble, I think, in November, and injured her neck or back or something of the type, and the local doctors couldn't do anything for her, and we sent her to a neurologist and a nerve specialist in San Diego, and they worked on her, and she has been under treatment by the local doctor, Dr. Powell — oh, the usual things that go along with a family ___." (Whenever the police reporter couldn't make out what Mr. Huscher had said, he wrote a long straight line to indicate "unintelligible.")

"She did have one serious illness last August. She had galloping pneumonia. She was in the hospital for 15 days."

"Has she been treated for any mental disorder?" asked the deputy.

"No," Carroll said, "nothing like that."

Carroll had already told the police, while they were walking through the house earlier, that his wife had threatened suicide. Majors remembered that, and he asked Carroll to tell him when and where those threats had taken place.

"Well, going back," Carroll recalled, "just for seeming no apparent reason, it was 'What good am I?' 'What's the use of this?' or 'What's the use of that?' which didn't add up, on subject matters. I can't tell you what the subject was about."

"I see. Did she state what type of suicide she would commit?"

"Well, it was always she was going to jump off the end of the pier."

"I see."

"I heard that so much — well, I shouldn't say 'so much,' but probably on as many as eight or ten times, like the story ___ didn't pay much attention ___. Just one of those things I considered just part of the conversation."

"I see. When were you folks married?"

"January 1934."

"And this little girl, the victim here, is the only child?"

"Only child."

"Is she your true child, or is she adopted?"

"No, we adopted her. We got her through the court. Down in Superior Judge Joe Schell's."

"At what age?"

"She was 16 months."

In the eyes of every police official who wrote about the case, Judy would not be their "true child." Carroll Huscher would be listed twice as Judy's "foster father" and three times as the "stepfather" in the police report. Only Gladys would refer to Carroll as Judy's father.

"I see," said the deputy. "Had the wife ever threatened to kill her?"

"No."

They talked about strychnine, how Gladys had asked him to buy some three or four months ago. During the interview, Carroll kept calling it arsenic, something Deputy Majors straightened out with him afterwards and then fixed in the transcript.

Carroll said Gladys wanted him to kill mice using her mother's technique. "Her mother had lived in this home for some ten years," Carroll explained, so he knew that old Mrs. Teeple spread the strychnine on a piece of bread and left it lying around for the mice.

"I guess about a week or ten days ago, I was out here," Carroll said, "and she said, 'I'm having a little trouble with them,' meaning the mice, and I said, 'Didn't you get them with that stuff?' and she said, 'You didn't give it to me,' and I said, 'I did give it to you,' " and Gladys told Carroll that she'd gone down and bought some more.

Carroll then had to describe his drive that morning, the startling fact of the newspapers at the curb, the moment that he shielded his eyes from the sun and looked into his daughter's bedroom.

The deputy listened. He turned to the coroner. "Now, Mr. Creason," said Deputy Majors, "is there any facts you want to go back over?"

Mr. Creason nodded. "Just one, briefly, Mr. Huscher," he said. "Can you offer any explanation or give any reason why your wife might have wanted to do your daughter any harm?"

Mr. Huscher must have been startled by the question. "What's your name?" he asked the coroner.

"Creason."

"There's . . . Pardon me. There's a dozen things go through your mind in a situation like this."

"Maybe I could make it a little clearer for you, Mr. Huscher. Has your wife and daughter been close?"

"No, they haven't been real close, and that was probably the reason she and I, in our separation.... I felt that the two of them just weren't good for one another. My mother felt the same way. In fact, I had received a letter from my mother less than a month ago stating the fact that she hoped I could get a place where I could take Judy and have proper supervision and discipline, and Judy and I both would be far better off."

"Have you and Judy been ___?" The transcript leaves out the end of the question.

"No."

"Is there any possibility that your wife might have resented your actions towards your daughter, ___ being close?"

"Well, I am sure — but I am afraid that was, in part, of it."

"You think there was a jealousy here between your wife and your daughter, then?"

"I'm afraid there was. Because I can see now, I can, I have seen just recently why the welfare department thinks it best not to let a couple over 35 years old, or women particularly over 35, have a child, a tiny child, because their patience are not as long, and we have had too much freedom up to that many years without a youngster. In other words, when a woman is 38 years old, normally she's 40 or 42 years old, 45 years old [Gladys's age when they adopted Judy], hell, she's got a family practically raised and half married."

"Have you and Mrs. Huscher ever conversed among yourselves that possibly she strongly indicated to you that she was jealous of the child? Has she ever ridiculed you for being so close to the child?"

"Well, I wouldn't say ridiculed, no, I wouldn't say ridiculed. But she felt, as I say, that maybe I wasn't strong in disciplinary problems as I should. She ridiculed me for that. She is a perfectionist and in her business, and having qualified in her particular line, which is home ec."

"Was she a schoolteacher?"

"Yes, she's a schoolteacher. She's presently employed as a schoolteacher, yes, in the high school, and she is a top-notcher, and she is a perfectionist. Well, she wanted the child to be just a grown, I mean, an adult teenager — a girl, in fact, a child growing up that young is just not that way. She thinks, 'Do it this way,' and the child wants to do it another. Now that was a conflict, I am trying to put over to you. As far as hatred, no, I couldn't say that."

"That's about all?"

"Have I made myself clear to you?" Carroll asked.

"Yes," said the coroner. "You have."

They weren't finished, though. There was still the suicide note. They had to sort out what it said and where Carroll had found it, and then later they'd try to figure out what it meant.

Carroll reiterated that he'd found the note lying on the pill bottles. He said his name was facing up. The detective asked Carroll to read the note aloud.

"'As I told you last October, I was too worried,'" Carroll read, although the word they eventually settled on was "weary." " 'And then to get the terrific shock after I had tried so hard, and maybe this is what you wanted?'"

Deputy Majors noted that this part of the letter was written in green ink. Then he asked Huscher to read the part written in red pencil, the part that was just "little scribbles."

"What does that say?" he asked Carroll.

"'Why you had stayed away,' this looks like. I can't make the next one out. Maybe you can." Huscher handed the note back to the detective.

"I can't," Majors said. "It looks like 'I think I could have some.'"

Huscher took the letter back and studied it. That didn't make sense to him, because there were still three words after "some." "'I think I could have come out of it,'" he offered.

"And then on the other side," Majors said, "it looks like it says, 'You tantalize me.'" Then Deputy Majors said something the reporter couldn't make out, and Mr. Huscher made an unintelligible reply.

"Okay, that's all then," Majors said.

It was two o'clock in the afternoon. There were funeral arrangements to think about. Carroll had to call his mother and his sisters. At some point, he would also have to tell the other woman, the woman he'd been seeing, the woman he had not mentioned.

Everything was different now.

He walked out the front door of what would never really be his house again, just as this would cease to be his town.

GLADYS

She was born Gladys Bowes Teeple on August 24, 1901, the third unwanted daughter of an unsuccessful Minnesota salesman and clothier. There were "severe financial problems," she told one of two court-appointed psychiatrists, which made children "unwelcome burdens." She grew up, she went to college, and she made her way west by teaching home economics, first in White Bear, Minnesota, and then in El Centro, California, where her sister Ruth was living. From there Miss Teeple went west to Oceanside-Carlsbad Union High School and was featured in the 1933-4 yearbook above the ominously fitting epigraph, "According to the situation."

When Dr. John Robuck and Dr. G.W. Shannon were asked to evaluate her sanity 23 years later, Gladys remembered this period of her life as sacrificial. She had "shouldered the responsibility for support of her parents upon leaving college when she first took employment as a teacher" in 1923. She said that for ten years she had supported parents who, in her recollection, had not wanted to support her.

But Ruth and Madalene, Gladys's older sisters, were helping, too.

"My grandmother lived with Ruth," recalled Elizabeth Sage Gord, who was Gladys's niece and Madalene's daughter. In later years, Gladys's mother did live with the Huschers in Fallbrook, but in the early 1930s, when Gladys's parents got what amounted to a geographical divorce, Eleanor Teeple left Minnesota and moved in with Ruth. Edgar Teeple, Gladys's father, stayed in Minnesota and lived with Madalene.

Elizabeth also recalled, fondly, that Aunt Gladys took a trip to Hawaii in those years and had a lovely time. That she had a set of silver monogrammed with a T for Teeple. That she was well-loved by the family.

Perhaps Gladys felt her own sacrifice more keenly, as the unmarried sister, the one who had to use her own salary, not her husband's, to support her parents. Or perhaps, sitting in jail and waiting to be tried for the murder of her daughter, she knew she needed to point out those occasions — numerous and difficult — when she had been a good daughter herself.

Gladys Teeple met Carroll Huscher in the fall of 1933, in the fourth year of the Great Depression. She was 32 years old and well on her way to schoolmistress spinsterhood, carrying around with her the recent advice (of a friend? a sister? a doctor?) not to devote herself to her parents, but to marry instead.

Carroll was six years younger than Gladys. He had dark hair that she liked and a promising business. At 26, he worked with his father at Huscher's Grocery, which in a time of nationwide want and failure, in a town of fewer than a thousand people, Fred E. Huscher and son had had enough cash or credit to enlarge. Right after the expansion, the Huschers had paid for a new storefront, new paint, and new wallpaper. It wasn't just the store either. Carroll Dean Huscher had gas and a car to drive to Idyllwild just for pleasure on New Year's Day. He'd had gas and a car to attend, with his friend Harry Palm, a party at the Hotel Del Coronado.

Gladys Bowes Teeple was short but not small, not lithe, not flapper thin. Where Carroll was hard and sharp, she was soft and pliable: soft nose, chin, ankles, and shoulders. Miss Teeple (*so old not to be married yet!*) had an oval face and deeply recessed eyes. She wore her dark hair marcelled. A woman who'd been her student in Oceanside, who became the wife of the contractor who built the house on Knoll Park Lane, said Miss Teeple was "very pretty, very attractive, better than average." Perhaps this helped her to attract a man six years her junior — Gladys was old, for a maiden, and Carroll was short, for a man — or perhaps they simply loved one another, found each other perfect in every way.

In any case, Carroll D. Huscher courted Miss Teeple for three months. When they married on January 13, 1934, they did so before a justice of the peace in Florence, Arizona, not in the pretty white clapboard church on the hill above Huscher's Grocery. Although the *Fallbrook Enterprise* recorded practically everything members of the Huscher family did (*Mr. and Mrs. F. E. Huscher celebrated their 25th wedding anniversary with a family dinner party on Sunday*), especially if it required a motor car (*Miss Florence Huscher accompanied Harry Palm to Idyllwild to enjoy the snow sports, and Mr. and Mrs. Fred E. Huscher and daughters Florence and Winifred drove to Riverside and San Bernardino, returning by way of Chino and Corona*), no notice of the marriage appeared there, no mention of their route home from Arizona, no party in honor of Carroll's new bride.

Within a year, Mrs. Gladys Huscher had become the homemaking teacher at Fallbrook High School, a job with spectacular facilities built by out-of-work men and New Deal dollars. Named the best rural high school in the state, it boasted a pool, an elegant Spanish-style classroom building, a separate home ec facility, a gymnasium, and something called the Girls' Practice House or Model Home, a place in which to iron, sew, cook, and entertain, a dollhouse built to human scale.

Gladys was the only married woman on the staff, which was fitting, since she was preparing young women for life, not examinations. The model home and home ec building stood high on the highest hill of Iowa Street, looking down on Huscher's Grocery, Mobilgas, Safeway, the stationer's, a smattering of houses, the baseball field. Through the large-paned windows of the home ec building, stocked with Singer sewing machines and featuring six aqua-tiled kitchenettes, you could see crows, black phoebes, white streaks of clouds, and the blue, un-Minnesota-like sky. They put on a musical that year, *Hearts in Holland*, that the students wrote all by themselves, and Gladys sat at the sewing machine for hours to make costumes.

The Huscher name was already known at Fallbrook High through Carroll's younger sisters, Florence and Winifred. In 1934, the painstakingly typed and mimeographed *Monthly Buzz* quipped, "Just Suppose That… The Spanish teacher were a Trademark instead of a Brand… The commercial teacher were a Faulsitt instead of a Truitt… Florence were a Waker instead of a Huscher," and so on through the surnames of the staff and student body.

It was the kind of joke the *Monthly Buzz* specialized in, but Gladys Huscher was a Waker, of sorts, rousing girls in middy blouses to the almost certain future: motherhood and domestic toil. Homemaking was a major in those days, a path you could chart on the forms you filled out each semester.

"The vocational homemaking and related courses are planned to help the girl of today not only to live as a member of her family group, but to live well," said the student information packet of 1936. "Through these courses the girl will learn interesting and approved ways of doing those things every girl wants to do in her home.

"In the course Homemaking I, the girl will study food preservation; selection, preparation, and serving of breakfasts and luncheons at home and for school; personal home problems and family relationships; factors influencing health; care of the body (skin, throat, mouth and teeth, hands and nails, eyes, nose, hair, and feet); simple first aid remedies; invalid cookery and tray arrangements; arrangement and care of a girl's room; use and care of materials suitable for shorts, brassiere, and a wash dress. She will also make shorts, brassiere, and a wash dress."

Having mastered invalid cookery, personal home problems, and the construction of brassieres, the Homemaking II student would construct a silk blouse and a wool skirt and study the acquisition of becoming footwear. Of course, there was also the baby's layette, child care, the selection of food to meet the needs of oneself and family, "and every day courtesies for harmonious individual, family, and community relationships."

Although Mrs. Huscher taught interesting and approved ways of doing those things every girl wants to do in her home, she produced no children.

The Girls' League, 1944, Fallbrook High.
Yearbook photo. Gladys on far left.

"We felt we could not afford it," Gladys told Dr. Shannon.

In 1939, after just five years of marriage, someone told Gladys to leave her husband.

"I was advised to leave him," she said, "but I loved him too much."

Carroll was president of the State Frozen Food & Butcher

Association that year, and Gladys had a nervous breakdown. She cried a great deal. She cried so much that she went all the way to Pasadena to see a psychiatrist, who diagnosed her with a term she remembered ever after: "involutional signs," the psychiatrist said, referring to the "regressive alterations of a body or its parts characteristic of the aging process; specifically, decline marked…in women by the menopause."

Gladys was just 38 years old. She went back to teaching what the school called "art and its relation to food, silver, dishes, and linens."

The war came, and Carroll became a noncommissioned officer. He was in charge of the Camp Pendleton commissary, receiving and issuing all food supplies — a million dollars' worth of groceries went through his hands every month. He had his work and he had Boots, his beloved half-Morgan/half-Arabian horse, and Gladys had her work. She taught girls in bobby socks to make Eggs à la Goldenrod, to serve their mothers from the left at the annual mother-daughter tea, to wear gloves, to wash gloves, to iron tablecloths, to sew pin-tucks into batiste.

The *Monthly Buzz* became the *Monthly Warrior*, and in the "What's Buzzin', Cousin?" column of October 1943, Frances Geyer joked, "My next stop was Homemaking I, where I found the Freshmen trying to poison themselves. Imagine, them offering me some of their 'delicious' food!"

Mrs. Huscher kept cooking; she kept sewing. Although one of her closest friends, Ruby Aaberg, would testify that Gladys had been mentally ill since 1939, the year of that trip to see a psychiatrist in Pasadena, Gladys worked hard and made a good impression. She helped the Girls' League decorate the gym for the spring dance, the fall dance, the spring dance, the fall dance. She helped them make a Fountain of Youth and a Horror House. Her nephew died in the war, Madalene's only boy. The war ended, and other boys came home.

With his wife's teaching salary — so sure, so dependable — Carroll could take a chance on a new venture: frozen foods. Huscher's Froz-N Foods was right there on Alvarado Street, three blocks from the high school, close enough that high school boys could run over in the Huschers' car and pick up meat for home ec classes.

But the Teeple women tended to break down at menopause, and Gladys already knew what that felt like, how it had gripped her in 1939. By the time the war ended, she was 44. She wore glasses. She'd become one of those women in the ads for Dr. Pierce's tonic, gazing at numbers on a blackboard: 43, 44, 45, 46…50.

> *Physicians call this period menopause. It is the dreaded change of life. Women should face this period with well-balanced health or dangerous symptoms may appear. This is the time when deficiencies in general health must be helped. Every woman approaching middle age should take Dr. Pierce's favorite prescription, Blended Herbal Tonic.*

Meanwhile, Dean was 38, no fatter than he'd been on their wedding day, a thin, small, dark-haired man who hadn't even begun to go bald. The *Fallbrook Enterprise* was full of babies and children, children and babies.

> *On Sunday, Mr. and Mrs. N.A. Waller and their children, Ann and Mary, and Mr. and Mrs. R.J. Beeman and their son, Bruce, drove to Palomar Mountain, where they had a delightful day. The children experienced their first snow.*

Every week, the *Enterprise* ran a syndicated column from Washington called "Memo to Mrs. Housewife," with tips such as, *Did you know that baby sweater frames can be purchased that will "grow" right along with his or her nibs? Preventing shrinking or stretching they come in adjustable sizes with a helpful booklet of washing instructions.*

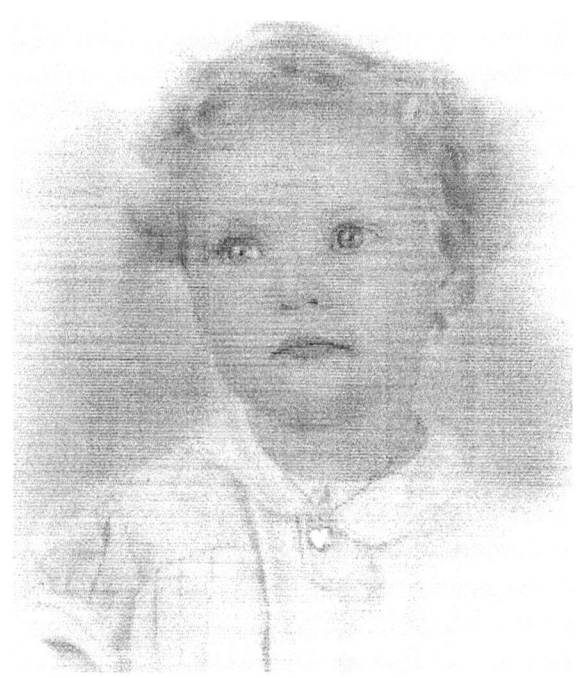

Judy Huscher, undated photo.
Judy was adopted around the age of 16 months.

In 1946, a baby came up for adoption, a beautiful blonde one-year-old girl. She was placed with a family in Fallbrook that already had three children, including 12-year-old Suzy Morris. Suzy thought she heard her mother say she'd sooner adopt Judy than let the Huschers have her, but there were already three children in the Morris house, and Mrs. Morris took in foster children to supplement the family income.

"Carroll fell in love with her," Suzy said. He saw Judy somewhere, perhaps in Mrs. Morris's arms when she came into Huscher's Froz-N Foods.

The welfare department thought it best not to let people over 35 adopt babies, but in 1946 or early 1947 (accounts of Judy's age at adoption contradict the dates given in various reports, and the official adoption record remains sealed) Judge Schell awarded Judy to Carroll Dean and Gladys Huscher, worthy, hardworking, childless people, a second-generation Fallbrook grocer (age: 39) and his Minnesota-born wife (age: 45).

Judy and Gladys with Lorraine Flippen
at Live Oak Park in Fallbrook

Not everyone in Fallbrook agreed with Judge Schell. Some, including the Morris family, thought the Huschers were too old. "It was politics," said the postman. "Carroll pulled strings. Out of the clear blue sky they adopted her."

Still, Judy became theirs, and for the first time in 23 years, Gladys stopped teaching homemaking in order to make home. The 1947 yearbook shows Gladys stirring something at the model house's model stove, a model mother in a button-up dress with three-quarter-length sleeves. Her students wrote the caption: "efficient and capable…fastidious but chic…digressive…now home practicing what she preached."

Gladys had a child to take to the Memorial Day picnic at Live Oak Park. Tree games for children, the egg race, musical chairs! Judy would be old enough for all of it someday, would be in her friend Elta's class at the grammar school, perhaps, could learn to sew and cook with her mother, to make shorts, a brassiere, and a wash dress.

Memo to Mrs. Housewife: Either the full or slim silhouette is stylish this year. But, ladies, they're both fitted closely to the figure, accenting a small waistline and the natural curves.

By Christmas of 1948, Judy was old enough for play school with Cal and John and Katie. In the photograph that someone else's mother kept (the names dutifully recorded on the back) little Judy holds a doll. She seems, in fact, to be a doll, a three-year-old girl-doll in a dark cabled turtleneck sweater, the corners of her red lips turned down, her eyebrows a neat pair of curves. Her face is pure and serious, perfectly round, wisps of hair escaping from two minutely cinched rows of braids.

Judy wears her hair the same way in another photograph, one in which Gladys and her friend Lorraine Flippen (who would die of polio in Mexico not too many years later) laugh together and help Judy to a picnic lunch. A glass tray of carrots sits on the table beside a huge tin pot. A silver-tipped thermos gleams like a silo. Lorraine's face is blurred with happiness, and Gladys looks efficient and capable, leaning over Judy to scoop something out of a jar, to help her dear little girl, her passage to the picnic, to the world she has taught as a sort of puppet show all her adult life. The trees of Live Oak Park are thick and dark behind her, casting gray shadows on the grass.

"She was an adorable little girl when they first got her, but they just didn't do well with her," said a former student. "She was completely out of hand." The woman who had taught everyone else how to care for home and children had received, in spite of rules and regulations, a child of her own, a beautiful blank slate, a living doll, but the older Judy got, the less teachable she was and the more unruly she became. People judged Gladys for that. *Now home practicing what she preached.* They were watching her all the time.

In 1949, when Judy was four, Gladys Huscher became severely depressed. She wanted to kill herself but didn't. That was the year Carroll Dean was president of the Chamber, the year he had his picture taken with Congressman Richard Nixon and a federal judge's wife and the chairwoman of the San Diego County Republican Central Committee.

Memo to Mrs. Housewife: Junior can now be tempted to brush his teeth with a new tablet dentifrice that tastes like candy. All you do is take the tablet, a sip of water, then chew and brush.

HOUSEHOLD GOOD

In September of 1950, Judy started kindergarten and Mrs. Huscher returned to Fallbrook High, her hair the color of iron, her smile determined. "Nothing lovelier can be found in woman," said her yearbook caption, "than to study household good, and good works in her husband promote."

Judy Huscher at preschool
(standing in the back, holding a doll)

In 1951, Carroll Dean Huscher helped fight the federal government for Fallbrook's water rights, and Fallbrook won. Judy went to school with her hair cut short, uncurled, unbraided—easier that way. She wore a frilly plaid jumper in Mrs. Jameson's class.

In 1952, Carroll Dean and Gladys (in a becoming dress, in a becoming hat) attended a dinner for William Knowland, state senator, where they were seated between a writer for the L.A. *Times* and the president of Bandini Fertilizer.

Judy entered Mrs. Gosnell's third-grade class in 1953 with Suzy Morris and Carlin Yokum. Her hair was chin-length, the bangs high above her eyebrows, her eyes far apart, and her nose quite flat. On picture day, she wore the dress with the big plaid collar.

"I felt sorry for Mrs. Huscher," said a graduate of 1955, "because, you know, they adopted Judy. And I think motherhood was not very natural for Mrs. Huscher because she just couldn't control this young girl. I mean, boy, she would just get so frazzled. I remember one particular prom, it was a Christmas prom or something like that because we were making soap out of Lux flakes and water. You know, making a lake out in front of the gymnasium, and Mrs. Huscher was there — that must have been part of her advisor thing — and Judy was just out of control. She was trying to kick the stuff we were making, and the girls were screaming at her. And I just remember how frustrated she was that she could not control this young lady. At all. And I couldn't either when I babysat. I mean, [Judy] would just tell me, 'No.'

"Judy was about, oh, I'd say, nine years old. Very spoiled. I hated that. I mean, I did not like babysitting for her. And my mother said, 'You should babysit for her. I said yes for you.' And I'd go, 'Oh, no!' You know, you'd tell her to go to bed and she'd say, 'I don't have to.' She was a little pill. She didn't think she had to do anything a babysitter told her to do, and I'm not real assertive, so it was very difficult for me."

"She was as mean as she could be," said a woman who was a year behind Judy in school. "I remember coming home in tears one day."

"She was unattractive, with red hair and missing teeth," recalled the son of a high school teacher. Growing up, he used to see Judy at meetings of the 50/50 Club, the youth group of the Methodist church. "She was always running, always wild. Today, they'd probably say she was ADD."

Judy became a Camp Fire Girl, attended the meetings at Live Oak Park and other girls' houses. She heard the talk about character, crafts, outdoor interests, and the annual peanut fund-raiser. She met with Firemakers, Woodgatherers, Trail Seekers, and Torch Bearers.

"As an adult, looking back on the girl I knew named Judy, I would say there was something wrong with Judy," said one of the Camp Fire Girls. "That doesn't mean she might not have grown up to be just fine. But as a child, there was something 'off' about her. She was too loud, she laughed inappropriately (at inappropriate times), and she seemed to enjoy hurting others. Having said that, I also can't remember a single specific instance as an example. One of my strongest memories is that I remember her teeth . . . I didn't like seeing them...because when she was going to be mean, she'd smile and show a lot of teeth."

A younger girl who saw her from afar at Live Oak Park also thought there was something wrong.

"I wonder what I really thought at the time, but looking back, what I recollected was that you just felt uncomfortable because she didn't seem to have any idea how to *do* among people. You felt sorry. There was something strange, something odd. She was in trouble. And you didn't feel she was mean at all. You just felt she was lost."

Judy turned ten. Along came the Slinky, Silly Putty, *Peyton Place*, and Elvis. Judy got a horse (she was a town girl, but Carroll was in the Rider's Club), and they tied it in the front yard. Or sometimes Judy tied it; sometimes she forgot, and the horse wandered off.

Gladys kept teaching and smiling.

"Mrs. Huscher, I remember," said a graduate of '55. "The first thing we made was Eggs à la Goldenrod — creamed eggs on toast. Mrs. Huscher was a wonderful person. She was always immaculately dressed. I don't know if she was quite in touch with the way things were in the '50s, but she was — we all liked her a lot."

With this student, Gladys talked affectionately about Carroll and Judy. "She used to talk about her husband and her daughter all the time."

"She was really in her element as a home ec teacher," remembered another girl from that class. "As a home ec teacher she was very demanding." Students starched and ironed the napkins and the tablecloth, two things that do as you tell them — what a relief that must have seemed.

"I remember setting the table, and folding the napkins, and the tablecloth had to be the same length on both sides of the table, and mine wasn't one time, and…she said, 'This will never do.'"

Boys, too, took her classes, learned to form a "family" of five and make white sauce and a stuffed, rolled roast. She'd give her keys to a boy she trusted and send him down to get the meat from Dean at the locker.

"When I was there, she had gray hair, kind of plump — she seemed old," said one of those boys. "Mrs. Huscher would send me after meat, and I'd get in the clunky old Dodge, and I'd go down to the meat place and get the meat. It would be ready for me — I didn't have to go into the freezer itself.

"Some kids did give her a hard time, but I didn't. I think she enjoyed some of the little jokes and pranks they pulled. I didn't pull the pranks. I had a granny. I respected older people. Yes, I remember Judy. She was a real brat. I saw her lots of times with Mrs. Huscher. Judy was always barking what she wanted. I guess Mrs. Huscher didn't know how to discipline her."

LOVE, LABOR, AND LAUGH

For most of Judy's life, she had not just one grandmother nearby, but two. Her father's mother, Evelyn Huscher Hibbs, lived in town (Carroll's father, Fred Huscher, died in a car accident before Judy was born), and Gladys's mother lived with them when she wasn't living with Ruth or in the Chula Vista Methodist home.

"After we had the child, I was happy," Gladys told Dr. Shannon, "but I had to go back to work. He has never made a living wage. He is not a good businessman. It bothered him when I had to have Mother live with us for a time."

For a time. This is how it seemed to Gladys, or how she wanted it to appear. Carroll, on the other hand, told Deputy Majors, "Her mother had lived in this home for some ten years."

The Huscher home had two bedrooms, one for Judy and one for Carroll and Gladys. There was no spare room. Gladys's mother had her own way of doing things, naturally. Like spreading a little strychnine on the piece of bread and putting it where the mice were.

In the fall of 1955, another person came to live with the Huschers, a live-in nanny. Gladys's mother was apparently elsewhere at that time. Although Judy was old enough, at ten, to help her mother — to set the table, vacuum the floor, wash the dishes — the Huschers didn't ask her to, or she didn't comply.

"She was very hard to manage," said a home ec student of Mrs.

Huscher's. "That was why they had a college girl to help out with taking care of her."

The college girl was Bette, a Fallbrook High graduate with impeccable credentials: student body officer, president of the scholarship federation, a member of the Girl's Athletic Association, class secretary for two years, two years in the house of representatives. *"Love, labor, and laugh,"* said her yearbook caption the year she left Fallbrook High, a phrase her fellow editors thought was perfect, though Bette wasn't quite sure.

Bette also took home ec, and she got along well with Mrs. Huscher, who liked things done properly, done well.

"My impression of her was positive," Bette said of Gladys, "i.e., she was very pleasant all the time, well-groomed, and seemingly a good 'role model' for a homemaker (I speak in terms of the '50s). For me, her class wasn't very helpful as I came from a family where the girls started housekeeping at age ten. However, I realized that there were many in the class that found it educative."

The summer after graduation, in June of 1955, Bette had gotten a job inspecting strawberries at the co-op on Hawthorne Street. The farmers were paid according to Bette's gradings, and since Mr. Huscher was one of the chief officers of the co-op, he'd noticed her, and it was he who approached her for the sitter job.

Bette came to live with the Huschers in their pale house, attractive by middle-class standards, no bigger or smaller than most houses in Fallbrook. "Mrs. Huscher had a sense for interior decoration of that period. She was very tidy. I do recall vacuuming the living room often."

Bette shared Judy's room, and in the evenings, Mrs. Huscher was always busy with her work or housework. She treated Bette with courtesy, let her know that she had confidence in Bette's ability to help out with the house and Judy, but Gladys did not at any time talk about her problems with Bette. "She had a veil of formality with me, always kind and never confiding her inner turmoils."

As for Judy, Bette said she was "a beautiful child, a little bit Shirley Temple with her golden locks. However, she was a handful, very strung out and unpredictable when she had a mood swing. I recall once when her parents were trying to help her with some homework and she refused to sit still and listen. I agreed to help her, and I had better success calming her down for about 20 or 30 minutes. Today, she would probably be diagnosed with some sort of learning disability."

To Bette, Mr. Huscher seemed very busy with his business affairs and community activities. Her sister heard bad things about him: other teenagers called him sleazy or slimy. Mr. Huscher made a remark to Bette, once, about a boy making out with her, and she thought that was in very bad taste. But Bette mostly felt neutral about him until the fall of 1956.

"One day, Mr. Huscher approached me and said he would have to let me go because 'I wasn't doing enough.' I was flabbergasted."

Although Mrs. Huscher had never indicated to Bette that anything was wrong, Bette said, Mrs. Huscher didn't intervene.

"I thought I earned my keep, as I was their maid as well as their sitter," Bette said. "When I was leaving, Mrs. Huscher said she was sorry that I was leaving, so I felt perhaps it was solely Mr. Huscher's decision."

Gladys Huscher mentioned Bette only twice in the surviving documents: a police interrogation and a psychiatric report. To Dr. Shannon, the female psychiatrist who interviewed Gladys in jail, Bette was simply "the high school girl."

"During the past two years [Mr. Huscher] has not been himself," Gladys told Dr. Shannon. "He wouldn't fix things around the house. The garage is a mess, and he hasn't done anything to clean it up. Two years ago he sold his locker plant and is in a new business with several other men. They process strawberries, and they are just getting on their feet during the past year. About one year ago, he moved out of the bedroom into the living room. I had to have a high school girl to take care of Judy and keep house for me. Of course, we didn't live a normal life, and he complained because I was cold but really I was just weary. All summer he was still sleeping out there. Mother came in July or August. Even though he has been making $150.00 per week, I had to pay all the bills. He has had another woman since April. When school opened last September, I was too ill to start, but I went back in October. I had wanted to quit, but he said, 'no' — that we needed the money."

Gladys mentioned Bette by name during an exchange with the police about strychnine bottles. "Where did you keep the strychnine in the house, Mrs. Huscher?" Deputy Majors asked. "That strychnine that you bought to kill the field mice with?"

"I don't remember," she said.

"Did you keep it in the house or in the garage?"

"I think it was in the garage. My husband wouldn't do nothing about the mice."

"Did you use some on the mice and get them?"

"Yes, I did."

"What did you do with the strychnine afterwards?"

"I don't remember."

"Don't you remember having it in the kitchen last Saturday night?"

"I didn't have it in the kitchen."

"Your fingerprints are on the bottle."

"They may be there, but I don't remember. Bette helped me get the mice too, because they were all over the house, and he wouldn't get them. He was too interested in somebody else."

That is all Gladys Huscher said about the girl who lived with her and slept in her daughter's room and ate dinner with them and folded their laundry and did their chores — an offhand remark that her fingerprints might have been on the bottle of poison that killed Judy. Of the possible reasons that a conscientious live-in nanny might be asked to go (jealousy, financial strain, a desire to stop performing imperfectly before a live audience), all seem possible but none provable. According to Carroll Huscher, the illness Gladys mentioned to Dr. Shannon (*When school opened last September, I was too ill to start*) was "galloping pneumonia," and Gladys was in the hospital with it for 15 days. It's peculiar that after an illness, when presumably Mrs. Huscher would have needed even more help, Bette was dismissed.

But Mrs. Huscher's suspicions about her husband's fidelity were very strong in the fall of 1956. She told Dr. Shannon that Dean promised to take her places on the weekends and then later refused, which made Gladys fear he'd spent time with another woman instead. Dean told her he was going to the far-off mountain town of Idyllwild, but she checked his odometer and saw that he'd traveled only 30 miles. She confronted him with this, saying a friend had seen his car parked at a certain place. He admitted he had been with someone else. At such a time would Gladys Huscher have wanted a beautiful 18-year-old girl near her husband? At such a time would Gladys have wanted anyone to see what was really going on in the home ec teacher's Model Home?

THE BLONDE

ubterfuge followed suspicion. Gladys began to spy on her husband, to try to "catch him in lies." Once, while the Huscher family was in a restaurant, Carroll excused himself to talk on the telephone, and Gladys sent Judy to eavesdrop.

In November, Carroll told Gladys he was going to a business meeting at the Fireside Inn in Escondido (the city where Carroll's mistress did, in fact, live, so this time there would be no discrepancy if Gladys checked the odometer). A domestic problem of some kind came up, so Gladys called the restaurant. The employee who answered the phone informed Gladys that there was no meeting to interrupt.

Gladys put down the phone. Then she picked it up again, calling everyone she could think of. She tried to find him, but she failed.

Like many women before and since, she waited up for him. At 3:00 a.m., when Mr. Huscher entered the house (the ornate dining room table, the vacuumed rug), he admitted that he hadn't been at a meeting.

"I pinned him down, and he admitted that he had a woman and told me her name. Next day I called her up very sweetly and thanked her for taking care of one side of my husband's life. She was surprised; she didn't know what to say."

Mr. Huscher's version of it, given to police on the day that he found Judy's body, was that he offered to move out in October because he couldn't satisfy Gladys in any shape, way, or form, but Gladys asked him to stay. Then, in December, Gladys suggested that Dean go ahead and move out. They went to see Charles Provence, the lawyer friend of Madalene's, and they worked out the terms of the divorce.

Divorce was still unusual in Fallbrook, although the national divorce rate was rising. A contemporary of Judy's, one who graduated in 1964, recalled that she didn't know anyone personally whose parents were divorced until a cousin's parents separated in 1959. Another, who graduated in 1963, said that when she was in high school, a divorcée in town was raped. The woman's name wasn't mentioned, but the ages and genders of her children were specified, permitting everyone in town to identify her.

"This woman was divorced (not acceptable), lived in a small rental house near the back gate to Camp Pendleton (clearly a 'wrong' place to live) and didn't have important friends, etc., in Fallbrook. Hence, she was fair game for the newspaper."

Since Gladys was the high school's model of motherhood, the woman entrusted to teach girls the most important lessons they learned at Fallbrook High School, divorce could not have been ideal. A graduate of 1955 said, when asked what she felt she was supposed to learn at Fallbrook High — not in her home ec classes, but in her entire high school education — "How to be a good wife, and how to cook and take care of the family."

Huscher Family Photo from Ahrend Studios:
Carroll Dean, Gladys, and Judy Huscher

To Carroll, Gladys seemed agreeable to the terms of the divorce, but she was consumed by jealousy. She drove from the house on Knoll Park Lane to the strawberry co-op, which was just one block east of Main Street. Carroll had started living there after the separation, probably since it was convenient and free. It was also very close to the center of town. The shopkeepers knew Gladys by name and by sight, as did their teenaged children. Nearly everyone in town, really, would have known who she was. Nevertheless, Gladys parked her car and walked up to the little block building on Hawthorne Street, where she tried to look through the windows. She tried to see her husband's lover, referred to in police reports only as "the blonde."

Gladys told Dr. Shannon that she had agreed to let Dean take care of Judy when Gladys went to visit Madalene, Ruth, or her mother in Chula Vista. Gladys had even agreed that Dean could take Judy with him when he went to visit the blonde, but it seemed deceitful to her later, and she told Dr. Shannon that it was.

"[Gladys] frequently referred to this other woman as an

unprincipled person and said, 'I couldn't stand the thought of Judy going to live with a person living in deceit.' "

Judy, meanwhile, liked the other woman, or she enjoyed the power of saying that she did. Judy said complimentary things to her mother about the other woman, about staying overnight there and having "nice times together."

This would have been especially galling since Gladys and Judy were not having nice times together. Judy was 12, nearly a teenager. She was as tall as her mother, though she weighed much less. She liked to run around outside, not to play like a girl. She was a tetherball ace at school. The only schoolmate who remembered her fondly — the only one who did not think there was something wrong with Judy — was the boy who shared a double desk with her, who shared with her the distinction of achieving less, academically, than other children and who was furthermore glad to hear the bell ring for the end of recess because that meant the end of Judy's domination at the tetherball pole.

She had always been this way, physical in the extreme. "I remember taking moving pictures of my oldest son's first birthday party," Gladys's niece, Elizabeth, recalled, "and under the table were these feet that were always moving." The feet were Judy's.

"Judy was a handful," said Elizabeth, who was 23 when Gladys adopted Judy. "Whenever they came to visit, poor Gladys, Judy was everywhere. And Gladys was always having to watch Judy to see that she didn't do what she shouldn't. I don't know that Dean knew how to handle her either."

When asked if Madalene and Ruth and their mother tried to tell Gladys how to handle Judy, Elizabeth couldn't recall.

"It's hard to tell someone how to manage her own child," she said.

When told that some people in Fallbrook had implied it was Gladys's fault that Judy was out of control, Elizabeth said, "They have?" Then she said, "It's true that Gladys wasn't emotionally prepared for a child like Judy."

But Elizabeth doesn't believe it was Gladys's troubles with Judy that led Gladys to walk into the garage and pick up two bottles of strychnine. "I think it was Dean that put her in a mental state to do what she did."

He wasn't really popular in the family?

"Not really. Of course, they accepted him because he was her husband."

TANTALUS

In Greek mythology, there's a favored king named Tantalus who wants to impress the gods with his devotion. He can think of no greater sacrifice than his beloved son, Pelops. He kills his son and offers him up, in the form of a stew, to the gods. The gods are horrified. They bring the son back to life and condemn Tantalus to stand forever in a lake. The water is all around him, but when he tries to bend over and drink, the water dries up. A tree of ripe fruit hangs over his head, but when he tries to pick it, the fruit swings away.

All through the winter, Dean came to the house. He came every day, twice a day, to feed a horse his daughter, at 12, was old enough to feed herself. Gladys saw him through the window, she saw him at the door. She saw him on weekends when they traded Judy back and forth. Always hungry, and always in sight of food. Always thirsty, and always standing in the receding lake. *If you had stayed away as you desired, I think I could have come out of it. You tantalized me.*

And yet when he was home with her, she wanted him to sleep on the couch. It's a paradox, a conundrum, two feelings that cancel each other out.

Toward the end of March, Gladys Huscher withdrew money from a joint bank account and placed it in her own account. She made a new will that excluded Dean. She and Dean had discussed the division of property on several occasions, but it still wasn't settled to her satisfaction. She would get the house and equity in the car but no part of the business, which according to Gladys was just beginning to show promise of a profit and which, according to Gladys, had been kept afloat for many years with Gladys's savings and inheritance.

On Friday, March 29, Gladys came home from school to find a letter from Charles Provence in the mailbox. It suggested she wait until after school was out — ten more weeks — to get the divorce.

"I was floored," she told Dr. Shannon. "I couldn't stand having him come every day and call Judy. It was very disturbing. I didn't see how I could pay the bills. I needed new teeth. On that afternoon I went to see the minister and told him all about it."

After confiding in the Reverend Stanley Smith, Gladys wrote a cryptic letter to her friends the Kelseys and Ruby Aaberg.

Josephine, George, and Ruby,

Please forgive me. You tried hard to help me. I hope God will bless you in more ways than one. Gladys — I tried and J. you know I did, but I was not equal to those cocky smirky looks and conversations, and no understandings or chance to work it out. Always chaperoned in our home.

Cocky smirky looks and conversations? Whose looks did Gladys mean? And who is the chaperone?

Perhaps the cocky smirky looks were exchanged by Judy and Carroll, who tantalized Gladys with the happiness and love they still shared, who were on their way to a life beyond Gladys, a life with the blonde. But the most likely chaperone is Carroll (Bette was gone by the spring of 1957, and Gladys's mother was elsewhere), and it's hard to see Carroll as both a watchful guardian, an escort whose job is to enforce propriety, and a conspirator exchanging cocky smirky looks with his daughter.

With no further elaboration, Gladys folded the letter and mailed it to the Kelseys on Stage Coach Lane.

On Saturday morning, March 30, Judy played with a girl named Jasmine, who said Judy's mother had called her mother and asked if Jasmine would please come over to play. Jasmine protested at first but then consented to go because she felt sorry for Judy, whose behavior made her unpopular at school.

"We were out in the yard, petting her horse, just hanging out," Jasmine recalled 55 years later, "and as usual she began to get really silly. I remember telling her I was going to go home if she didn't stop. She did slow down.

"Soon her mom called us in to have some ice cream. It was chocolate. We were sitting at a table by the window when her dad stopped just outside and talked with us. He was so nice, and we three chatted, and then he went on to finish what he was doing. He was wearing his large straw hat and had his glasses on.

"Judy and I continued talking about small stuff and suddenly she bent over her dish of ice cream and moaned, like in pain. I said, 'Are you okay?'

"After a second, she sat up and said she was, and we continued our conversation. A few minutes later, she again bent over, grabbing her stomach, and loudly moaning as in pain. I said again, 'Are you sure you are okay?'"

This continued until Jasmine offered the only suggestion she could think of, which was that maybe Judy should go to the bathroom. Jasmine sat and watched Judy's ice cream melt. Mrs. Huscher came into the room a short while later, said Judy didn't feel well, and that Jasmine's mother was on her way. Mrs. Huscher took Judy to her bedroom, and Jasmine waited outside by herself for her mother's car.

That afternoon, Judy must have recovered enough to leave the house. She stayed with her father at the strawberry co-op, and Gladys went to Safeway, picking item after item off the shelves for the cakes and roasts and sauces of her home economics classes, which were now taught at the raw new high school south of town, far from the Girls' Practice House and the aqua-tiled kitchenettes, from the bird's-eye view of the unlimited future.

"I was all in Saturday night," she told Dr. Shannon. "In the back of my head was the thought of suicide." She had thought about suicide so often in the past two years that she had saved four bottles of sedatives.

"Every day in school I had been wondering what was to happen. I put on a bold front, but inside I was weary and worried and it took three Seconals every night to get me to sleep."

She picked up Judy at 4:30 and came home. There was supper to think about. She made ground meat and string beans, the yellow ones. Perhaps Judy went out to play while Gladys cooked, because as Gladys recalled it, "Judy came home late, had her supper, then her father called her. She sat and watched television and had her ice cream on a TV tray."

In those days, you could watch three channels in Fallbrook: 6, 8, and 10. Judy always watched *The Jackie Gleason Show* at eight o'clock. The ice cream that she ate for the second time that day while she watched "Mr. Saturday Night" was endlessly discussed in the police interrogations.

"Did Judy have any ice cream or any chocolate before she went to bed?" the deputy asked Gladys.

"I think she did," Gladys said.

"What was it? Do you recall?"

"I think she had chocolate ice cream."

"What did you have?"

"I didn't have anything."

"Did you drink anything?"

"No."

"You didn't drink any coffee?"

"I had Sanka."

"You had some Sanka coffee?"

"Yes."

"Did you take any pills with your coffee?"

"No."

"Do you recall giving the ice cream to Judy?"

"No."

"Did she eat ice cream before or after she got in bed?"

"She ate it watching television."

"Did you fix the ice cream for her?"

"No, she fixed it herself."

"What did she eat it out of?"

"The carton."

"Right out of the carton?"

"Yes. Majors, I don't know who you are."

"I'm with the sheriff's office, Mrs. Huscher. Did they tell you what happened to Judy?"

"No."

Judy ate the last of the ice cream right out of the carton, put on her pajamas, and either did or didn't put on the black elastic head brace she was supposed to hook onto her braces and wear in her sleep. She went to bed in a room that was now her own — no college girl, no grandmother. Two dozen figurines kept her company: hippo, deer, bird, owl, dog, squirrel, and camel, all of them known, all of them mute. She lay down near her tiny vases and souvenir spoons.

Gladys collected all the money she had in the house and put it in an envelope. It was $50. She left Judy asleep in bed, alone in the house. She got in the Dodge, drove downtown in a night absolutely unlit by the moon, and mailed $50 to her mother. Then she drove home. She shut the car door and went into the house. Then she walked into the garage, which was a mess, filled with things Dean couldn't store in the strawberry plant, his papers and his desk, and she fetched two bottles, each as thin as her little finger. The bottles were brown. You had to sign for them at the pharmacy. He had to know you, the pharmacist did, and of course he did know Gladys.

She got the pills too, the four bottles of prescription medicine she'd been saving for a night like this. She had Seconal for sleeping, belladonna for her bowels. There were red ones and white ones, tablets and capsules. These she would take herself.

But first (or was it first? she told the story differently each time), she stood at the stove. She mixed bitter strychnine with sweet cocoa and milk in a pan. She stirred it, but she couldn't remember, later, if she heated it.

She would have known that it killed not only mice, but dogs too, killed them all the time in Fallbrook. Strychnine was also used to treat atonic constipation during Gladys's lifetime. This medicinal strychnine, called strychnine sulfate, was sold, like strychnine alkaloid, in brown bottles. The bottles were larger and were shaped differently. A bottle labeled "strychnine sulfate" described the adult dose as "one tablet as directed by a physician." It also said, right on the front, POISON.

Gladys stirred the cocoa. She poured one whole bottle of powdered strychnine alkaloid in, and she picked the labels off both bottles. She didn't throw the incriminating labels into the trash, where the empty carton of ice cream and an empty mayonnaise jar were. Nor did she burn them, flush them down the toilet, or do anything else that would have delayed the discovery of poison in Judy's body. She left the torn pieces that said "poison" in the sink, and she walked toward her daughter's room.

STRYCHNOS

The Huscher house still sits on a quiet street. It has the air of the innocent past about it, the late '40s and early '50s, when Knoll Park Lane was called "Principal Row" and women wore aprons with high-heeled shoes. The house has doubled in size since Judy lived there, pushed out backwards to give everyone more space. A software developer rents it because it's large enough to be both home and office, and he has yet to find the right use for Judy's room, so it remains empty. The kitchen that Mrs. Huscher badgered the contractor about, wanting it just so, was ripped out during the renovation. There's a plain, outdated wet bar in its place — no stove, no freezer.

Still, the doors and windows are original. The window glass in the rear bedroom is the glass that Mr. Huscher tapped on with a 50-cent piece, the glass that was cold beside Judy when the poison started to work.

Strychnine is the principal alkaloid in the seeds of a tree native to India called *Strychnos nux-vomica*. Although *nux-vomica* has been translated to mean "emetic nut," and although everyone who saw Judy's bed that Sunday morning feared the chocolate stains were of that nature, strychnine does not induce vomiting. The word "vomica" actually means depression or cavity, a feature of the strychnos seed attributed by legend to the fingerprint of the Creator.

"I'm with the sheriff's office, Mrs. Huscher. Did they tell you
what happened to Judy?"
"No."
"You knew she got sick Saturday night, didn't you?"
"No."
"You don't recall her being sick?"
"No."
"Do you recall taking the toilet tissue in the bed to her when
she threw up?"
"No, I didn't know she threw up."
"Did you take the spoon into the bed, or did she take it in
with her?"
"She didn't take the spoon into the bed with her. She ate at the
television."

Strychnine works fast. It could have awakened Judy within 15 minutes. The muscle spasms it causes are uncontrollable and total, affecting the face, arms, legs, throat, lungs, and heart. Noises and lights — the barking of a dog, the glare of a bulb — can trigger violent contractions.

"Did they tell you what happened to Judy?"
"No."
"You know she got terrifically sick that night, don't you?"
"No, I didn't know."

It probably started with Judy's legs and arms. They stiffened and extended themselves, threw themselves out in a violent unbending. Then she had her first tetanic convulsion, meaning her body arched and hyperextended until only the crown of her head and the heels of her feet were touching the bed.

The undersigned also observed what appeared to be the same chocolate substance on a small electric heater next to the toilet. On the water closet, behind the toilet, there was a black elastic head brace, which the victim's foster father stated the victim wore to bed nightly and which hooked onto the braces of her teeth. The chocolate substance on the electric heater and the child's head brace on the water closet both tended to indicate to the undersigned that the child had gone to the bathroom, where she got the towel and the toilet paper found in her bedroom, probably after becoming sick.

Deputy Majors believed that Judy "got sick," as did nearly every official who came to the house. That may be, however, because people had the erroneous idea that strychnine was an emetic. No one ever explained satisfactorily why Judy's head brace was on the water tank. The first possibility is that Judy never put it on before she went to bed. Maybe she forgot, or maybe she hoped she'd get away with skipping a night. The second possibility is that, as the officers speculated, she felt sick and walked to the bathroom, where she took off her head brace and threw up, and then took the toilet paper and the towel back to bed with her. The third possibility is that Gladys helped Judy remove her head brace when she brought in the cup of hot chocolate and the spoon. In that case, Gladys could have left the head brace on the toilet tank when she was done. But Gladys said that Judy was asleep, and it's hard to understand how Judy could remain asleep through so much activity.

"Didn't they tell you Judy passed away?"
"No."
"You knew she did, didn't you?"
"No, I didn't know."
"But you knew she would when you fed her ice cream with strychnine in it?"

"I didn't feed her. She ate. She had her ice cream while she was watching TV."

"Mrs. Huscher, now, look," said Deputy Majors. "You aren't telling me the truth on everything."

"Yes."

"You are?"

"I think so."

"I don't think you are."

"What's the matter?"

"You are not telling me about the pills you took nor about what Judy took that night before she went to bed."

"Judy took chocolate ice cream. She always likes chocolate ice cream. Her daddy knows that."

"Did she have anything else?"

"Not that I know of."

"Did she have some hot chocolate?"

"No."

All voluntary muscles, including Judy's mouth and eyes, were in full contraction. Her diaphragm contracted too, as did her throat and stomach muscles. She tried to draw breath, but she couldn't. She was absolutely conscious, more conscious than she'd ever been. "The patient is extremely apprehensive and fearful of impending death, as he awaits the next tetanic spasm."

"Do you know what happened to Judy?"

"No."

"Didn't anybody tell you?"

"No."

"I just told you, didn't I?"

"Yes."

"What did I tell you?"

"You told me she had died."

"That's right, and..."
"I didn't know."
"Aren't you really sorry?"
"Certainly I'm sorry."
"Do you wish you would have died also?"
"No."
"You didn't mean, then, for both of you to die? Just her?"
"I didn't mean for anybody to die."

If Gladys had already taken 50 belladonna pills (as she told one psychiatrist) or if she had taken one-fourth of a bottle of belladonna and a large number of sleeping pills (as she told another), she might have been poisoned by the time the strychnine began to throttle Judy. Belladonna is not a sleeping pill, but it contains an alkaloid, scopolamine, that can be used to induce drowsiness and dreamless sleep. Belladonna poisoning can cause delirium, psychosis, fever, flushed skin, dry mouth, dry skin, dry eyes, and pupils so dilated that bright light causes severe pain — a state described in *Alice in Wonderland* as "mad as a hatter, blind as a bat, red as a beet, hot as a hare, dry as a bone." An overdose of Seconal can cause staggering, blurred vision, impaired thinking, slurred speech, impaired perception of time and space, slowed reflexes and breathing, and reduced sensitivity to pain. Whatever the mixture of capsules and tablets, once they dissolved and began to move through her blood, Gladys Huscher was no help to anyone.

Judy was alone. Only the figurines, glossy and helpless, were watching as the convulsions came. *Hippo, bird, deer, owl.* Judy could do nothing to prevent her muscles from stretching her out in the full-body equivalent of a childbirth contraction. *Hippo, bird, deer, owl.* She couldn't breathe, and she was in searing pain. She had no idea why. It was the middle of the night. She had a spoon in her hand, and how it got to that balancing point on her lips no one will ever know. She died the way mice die in garages and pantries, as coyotes die in hilltop groves. No one heard her, and no one came.

At 1:00 p.m. on Sunday, March 31, Deputy Bob Majors walked into the Huscher house, having driven from downtown San Diego. He included the following note in his description of Judy's body:

In bed with her were three teddy bears...

TINY SHIPLEY'S HOSPITAL

Cars came and went all day on Knoll Park Lane. An ambulance took Mrs. Huscher to a little Spanish-style house on Main Street. Officially, it was Fallbrook Hospital, but everyone just called it Tiny's or Tiny Shipley's, after the diminutive nurse who ran it. Dr. Powell delivered babies there, Lionel Gray had entered into rest there Thursday, and now, in one of its small rooms, Mrs. Huscher was placed under watch. The nurses must have known her already, having seen her through the bout with pneumonia last fall. She was different now, though, from that innocent patient. She was a woman who had killed her own child.

Judy's body remained in bed with the teddy bears until she had been photographed by Sergeant Stables and Coroner Creason. Then she went by ambulance to Berry-Bell mortuary. At 5:40 p.m., Mr. Bell called Deputy Jim Moore to say that he and Dr. Fairchild had removed Judy's pajamas and put them in a brown cardboard box. Jim Moore drove over right away to pick them up and carried them down the street to the sheriff's office. That very night, a team of San Diego deputies made the long, dark drive to Fallbrook — a 90-minute trip each way — to fetch that box.

On Main Street, lights dimmed at the Mission Theater and the audience heard, for the first time, the thrumming of violins at the start of *Oklahoma!* Gordon MacRae fell in love with Shirley Jones.

The undertakers stood next to Judy as Dr. Fairchild, the autopsy surgeon, made "the usual Y incision." "In opening the chest, I find the lungs are only partially expanded with air… The heart is normal in size… On opening a window in the calvaria, I find the veins over the superior surface of the brain are distended with blood." Tiny parts of Judy were excised and labeled so they could be examined microscopically. Staring at the evidence, the coroner noted that her ovaries were immature.

Someone called the Morris house that night, knowing that Mrs. Morris had once tended and fed and loved Judy, had wished to adopt her years ago. Suzy Morris, the oldest child, had graduated from high school three years earlier and moved away, but she was home for a visit when the phone rang. "It was a Sunday," she said. "We were getting ready for bed." Her mother hung up the phone and said, "Gladys has murdered Judy."

Sometimes the wind picks up in Fallbrook and blows things to pieces. On Monday, April 1, Mrs. Margaret Slate received an early-morning phone call asking her to substitute in the high school home ec department. The hospital matron obtained a urine specimen from Mrs. Huscher for drug testing. A wind blew hard across the bare ground around the new high school. In people's yards, the wind knocked branches out of eucalyptus trees and bent TV antennas in half. Lemons and limes rained down. Orange blossoms flew like snow. Sheets circled clotheslines and towels ripped free. Downtown, the wind caught hold of the back door to Reader's Mercantile and smashed it. A whirlwind burst open the front door of Glad's Flower Shop, rocking potted plants and hurling imported glass plates to the floor.

On Stage Coach Lane, the mailman delivered a letter to the Kelsey house.

Josephine, George, and Ruby,

Please forgive me. You tried hard to help me. I hope God will bless you in more ways than one. Gladys — I tried and J. you know I did, but I was not equal to those cocky smirky looks and conversations, and no understandings or chance to work it out. Always chaperoned in our home.

Josephine opened the letter, read it, and showed it to her husband, who threw the envelope away. Josephine called Ruby Aaberg, a real estate saleswoman and grower of prize roses. It's possible that both of them had already read the article on the front page of the *San Diego Union* that morning: "Girl Dies of Poison, Fallbrook Mother Ill." Josephine and Ruby talked about the letter, but they didn't call the sheriff.

As the wind smacked things around, Deputy Majors unlocked the house on Knoll Park Lane. He walked through the empty house collecting evidence: one soiled pillowcase, one soiled bed pad, one soiled towel. He removed a roll of toilet tissue from the bathroom. He picked up the teaspoon that had lain on Judy's lips and had been dusted for fingerprints. He picked up everything else that might make the sequence of events clear.

"From the dining room table, five pill bottles." The coroner described only four: "Four prescription bottles on the dining room table: Bottle #1, 1585, issued by Dr. Powell, contains 15 small white tablets; Bottle #2, 535550, issued by Dr. Powell, contains 18 red tablets; Bottle #3, 239796-H, issued by Dr. Powell, contains 7 white capsules; Bottle #4, 212970, issued by Dr. Powell, is empty."

Deputy Majors continued to move about the room. "From the dining room floor, one piece of paper, on which Mrs. Huscher's head was lying." Two white pills that had fallen to the floor. A red pencil and a green ballpoint pen, both used by Mrs. Huscher to write the note. "From the kitchen, rolled up pieces of paper from the sink, which was believed to be the labels from the strychnine bottles. Two strychnine bottles. One aluminum pan."

In Encinitas, a city on the bluffs overlooking the Pacific

Ocean, a woman called out to Bette, Judy's former nanny. Bette had come to live with her as a companion when the Huschers let her go. She told Bette what had happened to Judy, the story that was spreading, person to person, house to house, town to town. Like everyone else, Bette couldn't quite take it in. The word she used to describe the feeling was "horror." She was horrified.

At Maie Ellis Grammar School, Judy's sixth-grade teacher told the class that Judy wouldn't be coming back.

Down the road at the high school, Mrs. Slate introduced herself, with a slight Southern accent, to each of Mrs. Huscher's home economics classes. She said she was the substitute. She drove over to the meat locker and picked up the meat that had been stored in a bin for the high school classes. The packages of frozen meat were rock hard, and once she unwrapped them, she saw they were white with freezer burn.

THE TUESDAY AFTER

On Tuesday morning, April 2, Carroll Huscher drove to the house, just as he had done every day when Judy was alive. He still had to take care of Judy's horse. It seemed to him, however, that the horse had stopped drinking. He wouldn't drink on Monday, and he wouldn't drink now. Maybe the water was poisoned too.

Carroll drove back to the strawberry co-op and called Deputy Majors. He told Majors he wanted someone to test the horse's water for poison, so Deputy Majors drove back to the house and collected water from the trough, water that would later prove to be perfectly fine.

That same morning, two visitors came to see Gladys. One was her older sister, Ruth, and one was her lawyer, Charles Provence. While they were there, Gladys Huscher regained consciousness.

Deputy Majors entered the room with two nurses and a shorthand stenographer at 1:20 p.m.

"Has there been somebody up to see you today?" he asked Mrs. Huscher.

"Yes," she said. "My sister came."

"Anybody else here?"

"No."

"Anybody come with your sister?"

"None that I know of."

Deputy Majors knew otherwise, but he didn't press further. "Are you in any pain now?"

"No."

"My name is Majors, Mrs. Huscher. I'm with the Sheriff's Department. I was the one who came up to your house the other day when you were sick and transferred to the hospital. Do you recall that?"

"No."

On that first conscious afternoon, Mrs. Huscher said she didn't recall Dr. Powell coming to the house, or Dean, either. She could remember the shopping trip to Safeway, and picking up Judy at the strawberry co-op, and what they ate for supper, and how Judy ate her ice cream right out of the carton. She emphatically denied poisoning Judy, and initially she denied attempting suicide.

"Do you recall writing a note to your husband when you were sitting there at the dining room table?"

"No."

"You must remember the note, don't you?"

"No."

"Can you see all right without your glasses?"

"I can't see without my glasses."

"Who is Dean?"

"My husband."

"And you wrote the note to him, don't you recall now?"

"No. I can't see without my glasses."

"What did you mean by 'terrific shock' that Dean gave you? In the note you talked about a terrific shock, Mrs. Huscher."

"He told me he was leaving me."

"How long ago had he told you that?"

"He told me last November."

"That's the shock you were talking about in the note?"

"I don't know. I didn't know he was leaving me."

"Why was he leaving you?"

"I don't know."

"Was it because you just didn't get along, or had he found some other woman?"

"He'd found another woman."

"That made you very mad, did it?"

"No, it made me very sad, because I wasn't aware we weren't getting along."

"Is that the reason you tried to do away with yourself and Judy that night?"

"No."

"What is the reason?"

"I didn't try to do away with ourselves."

"You didn't?"

"No."

"Do you recall having strychnine in the house?"

"No."

"No?"

"No."

"We must know the facts now, Mrs. Huscher."

"Yes."

"Do you want to rest a little while, and then I will talk to you later?"

"No."

"You're all right to talk now?"

"Yes."

"Do you recall putting strychnine in the food?"

"No, I didn't. She ate the chocolate ice cream herself, she really did."

"Did you take any of the strychnine, or did you just take the pills?"

"I didn't know I took the strychnine."

"You don't recall taking the pills you got at the drugstore?"

"I don't know."

"Getting back to this note you wrote, Mrs. Huscher. I will read it to you if you want me to."

"Yes."

"Okay."

"You mean the one about the shock?"

"Yes."

"Well, I told you that it shocked me terribly."

"Well, let me read this to you. Can you understand it now if I read it to you?"

"I told you that. It's going on with teaching, and I asked if I could quit, and he told me no, I couldn't quit. I had been sick with pneumonia and didn't want to do any more teaching."

"But Dean didn't want you to quit?"

"No."

"It goes on to say, 'And then to get the terrific shock after I had tried so hard.' That was for another woman?"

"Yes."

"Then it says, 'Well, maybe this is what you wanted.' What did you mean by that?"

"I don't know."

"Did you mean that what you thought he wanted was you and Judy out of the way?"

"I don't know."

"What did you mean, then?"

"I don't know."

She told Deputy Majors that she wanted Dean to thank their friends the Johnsons and Rileys because she hadn't seen them all weekend, not because she would never see them again. She denied so many things that Deputy Majors became impatient.

"Did they inform you when the funeral would be?" he asked.

"No," she said.

"You know what funeral I mean, don't you?"

Mrs. Huscher said, no, she didn't.

The interview concluded with the icy exchange about whether or not Gladys was sorry that Judy had died.

"Aren't you really sorry?"

"Certainly I'm sorry."

"Do you wish you would have died also?"

"No."

"You didn't mean, then, for both of you to die? Just her?"

"I didn't mean for anybody to die."

"Okay, Mrs. Huscher. Now I'm going. Maybe see you later, I don't know. And next time you probably will be feeling better, and then you can tell me all the truth?"

"I hope so."

It was 1:50 p.m. The interview had lasted 30 minutes, and Deputy Majors was leaving Tiny's hospital without a confession. He had evidence in the works, of course, the urine samples, the autopsy, the fingerprints, the scraped-off labels, the red pencil, the green pen, but he had no confession.

That evening, however, something happened. Ruth Teeple Reid, Gladys's sister, called Deputy Majors and told him that she had talked to Gladys "at great length" that Tuesday morning. Ruth told Deputy Majors that Gladys had admitted to her and Chuck Provence that she'd poisoned Judy intentionally and had taken sleeping pills in order to kill herself.

WEDNESDAY

The next morning, Deputy Majors was doing detective work in Fallbrook, talking to people who knew the Huschers. He got an anonymous tip that somebody in town had received a letter from Mrs. Huscher on Monday morning. The person who had received the letter, said the informant, was one of Mrs. Huscher's closest friends. Deputy Majors called Carroll Huscher and asked who this could be. Carroll said it was either Ruby Aaberg or Josephine Kelsey.

Deputy Majors called Ruby Aaberg first. Ruby didn't especially want to talk about the letter. She hesitantly admitted that a letter had been received, but not by her, personally. The salutation had included her name, but the letter had been received, she said, by the Kelseys. Ruby asked Majors not to give this information out.

With these two new pieces of information, Deputy Majors proceeded in a different mood to Tiny's Hospital. He arrived a few minutes before noon on April 3, while Margaret Slate was teaching classes that had heard, by now, why Mrs. Huscher wasn't in school. Deputy Majors brought witnesses into the hospital room: just Beatrice Tassey, this time, and Mr. Edwin C. Waltz, the stenographer. But Deputy Majors told Mr. Waltz not to write down the conversation unless Mrs. Huscher gave him permission.

*Having this information, the undersigned [Deputy Majors]
on April 3, 1957, in the second interview with Mrs. Huscher,
informed her that we wished her to tell us the same story she
had told her sister on the day previous. She at first denied
that she had told her sister these facts. However, during the
interview, the undersigned informed Mrs. Huscher that we
could, if she wished, have her sister come to the hospital and
refresh her memory regarding what their conversation was on
the day previous. Mrs. Huscher replied that she did not wish
to do this as her sister would probably be busy.*

Gladys began to talk. As Deputy Majors heard, at last, the words
he wanted to hear, the words he had been trying to summon from
Gladys Huscher, he tried to turn on a Dictaphone in his head,
tried to remember every word so that he could reconstruct the
unrecorded and thus unprovable confession he was about to hear.

"Why did you put the strychnine in the ice cream?" Majors
asked.

"I didn't put it in the ice cream," Gladys said.

"What did you put it in?"

"I put it in some chocolate. I don't know why I did it."

"You don't know why you did it? Wasn't it because you wished
to kill the child and then commit suicide?"

"Yes," Gladys said. "I did it so the other woman wouldn't be able
to have her if I died."

"Was this the other woman, the blond woman, who your
husband was seeing in Escondido?"

"Yes."

"Is that the reason you separated? Because Mr. Huscher had
found another woman?"

"Yes," Gladys said, and she broke down. At the mention of the
other woman, she began to sob.

"Who is this woman? What is her name?"

"I promised I would never tell who she was. You can ask him. He'll tell you."

"Where did you get the strychnine from that was brought in the house that evening?"

"From the garage."

"Did you bring it into the kitchen?"

"Yes."

"How much strychnine did you put in the chocolate drink?"

"I guess I put a whole bottle in."

"Was it mixed hot or cold?"

"I don't know. I don't remember."

"Did you mix it in an aluminum pan?"

"Yes."

"Did you take the chocolate drink in to Judith, who was in bed?"

"Yes."

"Was the chocolate on the bed sheets from Judy throwing up?"

"She didn't throw up. I spilled it on the bed."

"Did you clean it up after spilling it?"

"I didn't clean it up."

"Do you know, definitely, that it was strychnine you placed in the drink for Judy and what it would do if she drank it?"

"Yes."

"Do you recall scratching the labels from the strychnine bottles so no one could tell what they had contained and then putting the torn labels into the sink?"

"Yes."

"Did you take any of the strychnine yourself?"

"No."

"What became of the strychnine which was in the other bottle?"

"I don't recall."

"Were both bottles full of strychnine?"

"No. Only one of them, and that is the one I put in the chocolate drink for Judy."

"Did you originally purchase the strychnine to be used in poisoning mice in the house and the garage?"

"Yes, he wouldn't do anything about it, but I did find out later he had also bought a bottle of strychnine to be used for this."

"Do you recall taking sleeping pills before or after giving the chocolate drink to Judy?"

"I don't know."

"Do you know what you were going to do when you fixed the drink for Judy with strychnine in it?"

"Yes."

"How many pills do you recall taking?"

"I don't know. There was two bottles of them there. How many did you find left?"

The coroner knew the answer to this question, and Deputy Majors may also have known, but he didn't tell Gladys how many were left or say that there were four bottles, not two. "Were those bottles both full?" he asked.

"Yes."

"Did you know what these pills were?"

"Yes. Sleeping pills."

"Isn't it true that you told your sister this same story yesterday when she was here, and also that you told her that Judy had told you that she had been out with her father when he was out with the other woman on a couple of occasions?"

"Yes."

"Is this the woman who you were referring to when you stated that you didn't want the other woman to have Judy?"

"Yes, I didn't want her to have Judy. Judy loved her father and it was all right for him to have her, but I didn't want the other woman to have her."

"Just why did you put yourself to sleep, Mrs. Huscher?"

"Because I loved him."

"And you didn't want to put yourself out of the way and leave Judy?"

"That's right. I didn't."

"Did you write the note addressed to Dean which was found in the house?"

"Yes."

"Was this note written before or after you had taken the pills?"

"I don't recall."

At some point, Deputy Majors also asked Gladys if she recalled writing a letter to any of her friends. Gladys said she didn't. In his report, Deputy Majors wrote that Mrs. Huscher seemed to "bear up" under his questions until the end, when Majors asked permission to go over the story again so that Mr. Waltz could write it down. Mrs. Huscher then began to sob. "I've already told you that," she said, and she didn't want any more questions.

Deputy Majors, Mrs. Tassey, and Mr. Waltz went into the next room. Together they reconstructed the conversation, with Mr. Waltz making rapid marks in his book. Then Deputy Majors went to the telephone. He called Sergeant Strange in San Diego and told him to call the deputy district attorney, Claude Brown, to obtain a complaint charging Gladys Bowes Teeple Huscher with homicide.

Mrs. Huscher told Deputy Majors and the hospital superintendent, Beatrice Tassey, that she wanted to see her husband. She hadn't wanted to see him before, but she wanted to see him now, she said, so she could forgive him.

While the district attorney was issuing a warrant for the arrest of his wife, Carroll Huscher was driving down Main Street to Tiny's hospital.

The People of the State of California vs. Gladys Bowes Teeple Huscher. "You are therefore Commanded, forthwith, to arrest the above-named defendant and bring her before me forthwith, at my office in the City of San Diego, San Diego Township, in said County of San Diego, to be dealt with according to the law."

Carroll Huscher parked his car, prepared himself, and walked in.

Their conversation was not, of course, recorded. It was their first encounter since Judy's death, and it's hard to believe that Carroll would have felt the need to be forgiven.

After an unmeasured period of time, Carroll came out of Gladys's room. He told Deputy Majors that Gladys had asked for permission to go to the mortuary because she wanted to see Judy. While Gladys was getting dressed for the trip, Carroll told Deputy Majors that Dr. Powell and a San Diego doctor had been treating Gladys for several months for injuries to the back of her neck and the base of her brain. She'd injured herself falling off a stool at Fallbrook High School, Carroll said. Maybe this had some bearing on the crime, he suggested. Maybe that's why she wasn't right in the head. He said this even though he had, three days before, answered in the negative when Deputy Majors had asked, "Has she been treated for any mental disorder?"

Gladys was finally ready to make her last drive down Main Street as a relatively free citizen. She went to the car with Mrs. Tassey, Deputy Majors, Mr. Waltz, and her husband. They drove past the familiar sights, past Leighton Harrison's pharmacy, Jo Reader's mercantile, Jack Geyer's laundry, Glad Kuhns's flower shop. The police car stopped at the corner of Juniper and Vine. She'd passed the mortuary a thousand times because it lay between her house and the high school, between her house and the meat locker, between her house and everything else. It was a small, white building with three sets of doors. "The Chapel of the Hills," it was called.

The mortuary is still there. Rooms have been added on, padding the sides and the back, but once you get through the new lobby, the old chapel is there, small and silent, lit by stained-glass windows. The light coming through the cream-colored diamonds, purple diamonds, brown pine cones, and green diamonds is muted. Fourteen high-backed pews wait beneath paneled walls and an open-beamed ceiling, facing the emptiness that precedes the bier. Behind that empty space is a cupboard that, when opened, reveals a hand-painted scene of Fallbrook hills and oaks, a tranquil, uninhabited vista before which another bier might sit on a busy day, locked in the dark, waiting for the next funeral.

On the day that Gladys Huscher walked past those 14 pews, Judy's coffin was open. A dress covered the Y-incision. Judy's hair and scalp had been carefully arranged to cover the cut on the back of her head.

"Why did it have to happen?" Gladys asked.

She didn't ask to stay for the funeral, Deputy Majors informed reporters. The Reverend Stanley Smith, the minister Gladys had visited in despair on Friday afternoon, conducted the services at two. Children were let out of school to attend, but not all of them came, and fewer still approached the casket. The boy who had shared Judy's desk all year, who had hit tetherballs back to her on sunny day after sunny day, stayed in his pew and did not look at her. Carroll sat in the family viewing room, a recessed annex beside the bier that allowed him to cry or stare in peace, unseen by neighbors, friends, or enemies. Then Judith Ann Huscher, aged 12, was cremated.

SAN DIEGO COUNTY JAIL, WOMEN'S DIVISION

Gladys approached the county jail's booking window at about the time mourners were leaving Judy's funeral. She wore her coat over her shoulders like a cloak, and she held up her hand as though she were making an oath or a vow. She looked solemnly down, not at the newspaper and television cameras.

Judy's friend Jasmine was sitting on the floor in front of her family's television when the news came on that night. It showed two men on either side of Mrs. Huscher, walking her down the marble steps of the courthouse. Jasmine watched with her mother as the reporter announced that Mrs. Huscher had killed her own daughter. "I thought my mom was going to pass out. She gasped loudly — so loud it startled me — covered her mouth with one hand, and placed her other arm over her stomach. I think she was thinking I could have been harmed."

The next day, the image of Mrs. Huscher as a murderess hovered in the hands of mothers and fathers all over the county. They lifted the morning paper, scanned the front page, and read "Mother Confesses Poisoning Daughter — Fallbrook Teacher Admits She Gave Fatal Chocolate Mixture to Adopted Child." The toast grew cold, and coffee steam floated up as they read the bizarrely detached question Mrs. Huscher posed beside her daughter's coffin: "Why did it have to happen?"

If any of the women who read the paper that morning had given birth to a female child out of wedlock 12 years earlier, the news would have had particular, sickening force. Judy's biological mother, identity unknown, could have read the details about strychnine and mice, her brain all the while doing mathematical calculations, the months and years since her baby became a county case.

Gladys's family, of course, saw the papers. Her sisters, Madalene and Ruth; her mother, Eleanor; her brothers-in-law; her nieces and nephews.

Her oldest sister, Madalene, was shocked by what Gladys had done, but "she was very supportive of Gladys," said Madalene's daughter, Elizabeth. "She wanted to go down to the jail and see her," but Madalene didn't drive, so she had to wait until Elizabeth, who was teaching and raising two young boys, could go. They went on Saturdays or Sundays.

"I remember the first time we went down," Elizabeth said. "Gladys was wearing red oxfords and a blue dress" — the jail uniform.

Gladys's mother, too, wanted to visit, so Elizabeth took her once. The Teeple family seems to have forgiven Gladys, as families will, and blamed her husband for what happened.

"I felt real bad," Elizabeth recalled, "except I understood because I remember Dean. He wasn't always supportive of her. He always wanted her to do things that she didn't want to do. He was a meat man, and he got very politically involved. And he wanted her to do what he wanted her to do. He had a mind of his own."

Gladys had told her family that she was afraid Carroll would take Judy from her. She told them that she changed the locks. This does not appear to be true, since Carroll successfully unlocked the kitchen door on the morning of Judy's death, but Gladys gave them the impression, just the same, that she had to protect herself from

Carroll, and they believed her.

Gladys's sister, Madalene Sage, and her husband, Warren, were sympathetic enough to hire an attorney for Gladys. Through them, Gladys obtained the help of Charles Provence, who had been her divorce attorney. When Provence wrote about the Huscher case in his autobiography, he was less sympathetic than Elizabeth. He implied, in fact, that Gladys would have been better off dead.

"Gladys Huscher, a school teacher in the Fallbrook area," he wrote, "poisoned her ten-year-old daughter and herself. When their bodies were found, it was too late to save the child, but unfortunately for her, her friends and relatives, they were able to revive Mrs. Huscher. She was charged with first-degree murder.

"She was a sister of a very good friend of ours, a nice lady, and she and her husband were very good and longtime friends of ours and of many of our Imperial Valley friends. We had been in a bridge group with them for many years. We didn't know the defendant socially, but I had represented her in her divorce case a short time before.

"When Mr. Sage [Gladys's brother-in-law] came to me and asked if I would help them and defend her, I didn't like the idea, but I could not refuse. The child had been adopted by the Huschers and there was some evidence that Mrs. Huscher was jealous of the loving relationship between Mr. Huscher and the child. In favor of Mrs. Huscher was the fact that her attempt to commit suicide was bona fide. She had taken plenty and in just a few minutes more would have been gone."

Provence said he realized from the outset that the only possible defense was insanity.

"There is a presumption of sanity," he wrote, "and the defendant must produce sufficient evidence to overcome this presumption, and prove her insanity by a preponderance of the evidence."

Provence hadn't tried a criminal case in 20 years, but he talked to people in Fallbrook, and these conversations convinced him he had a "good case of insanity." He didn't want to try the case alone, however. He asked a criminal lawyer named Eddie Langford, who was "in court almost constantly," to be the expert on criminal procedure and technicalities so that Provence could focus on proving insanity.

At least one person thought Langford was a peculiar choice if you wanted your client to walk away after the trial. One of the court clerks asked Provence why he associated Eddie Langford with the case. " He's just a ticket to San Quentin," the clerk said.

Provence said he didn't think Langford was "that bad." He told the clerk that insanity was the issue, but Provence did wonder, later on, how Langford could prepare for so many cases at once. According to Eddie Langford's son, Perry, Langford was famous for taking notes in a tiny notebook — 1 inch x 2 inches — that he could keep in his pocket. "How can you talk to all those witnesses?" Provence asked.

"Hell," Langford said, "I don't have to prepare for trial. I just depend upon the weakness of the prosecution."

On April 22, the *San Diego Union* ran stories about not one but two mothers accused of killing their daughters: Gladys Huscher and Amelia Steward. Amelia Steward had allegedly stabbed her three-year-old daughter 39 times. The district attorney was seeking the death penalty in Steward's case, and Steward had entered a plea of not guilty by reason of insanity. Gladys Huscher, the article said, had not yet entered a formal plea, but that was exactly the plea Provence had in mind for her.

Provence apparently surprised Gladys when he entered the plea at her preliminary hearing.

"You mean you think I am crazy?" she asked him when the hearing ended.

"No, not at this time," Provence said.

Although Provence didn't recall it in his memoir, the hearing was the only time when Gladys reacted to Judy's death in a way that readers might recognize as sane. The *Fallbrook Enterprise* reported on April 25 that Gladys "broke into sobs when Deputy District Attorney Claude Brown introduced pictures of the girl."

While Provence set about proving that Gladys had, in the past, been crazy, Gladys assumed the same role in jail she'd held in Fallbrook.

"She was teaching a prostitute, Ruth, how to knit," Provence wrote. "When Ruth let go with some top-line vulgarity, Gladys said to her, 'Now, Ruth, if you are going to use language like that, I won't let you use my needles, and I won't teach you.' "

Friends and acquaintances, meanwhile, rallied to Gladys Huscher's aid in the only way they could. They called Provence and told him stories about "unusual conduct" and "aberrations" that convinced Provence that Gladys was "off her rocker."

"I asked them to get me names of similar witnesses and incidents," Provence wrote, "which they did."

At least one Fallbrook teacher, Harry Vix, visited Gladys in jail, and his son recalled that Gladys said to him, "Harry, what is it they say I've done?" The Vix family believed not that Gladys had gone insane but that she was innocent. They wondered if the circumstantial evidence didn't point at another killer.

Although it makes no particular sense, "much was made at the time of how a home ec teacher would know how to poison someone," said Gary Vix, who graduated in 1961, four years after Judy's death. "But Carroll owned a meat locker, and he would have had knowledge too." Furthermore, he sold ice cream.

Deputy Majors had also considered the possibility that the poison was in the ice cream carton, although it doesn't seem that he suspected Carroll of putting it there. Among the items Deputy Majors removed from the Huscher house for laboratory testing were the empty ice cream carton from the kitchen trash and bits of congealed ice cream found on the refrigerator tray. He submitted these to the lab, which reported them free of strychnine.

AN INTERVIEW WITH DR. SHANNON

In May, the rain set records in Fallbrook. The Camp Fire Girls, minus Judy Huscher, got together for the annual awards ceremony, honoring the Firemakers, Woodgatherers, Trail Seekers, and Torch Bearers. The Reverend Stanley Smith wrote a sermon called "The Land of Milk and Honey" and led his worshippers in the prayer of confession:

> *Our Heavenly Father, who by Thy love hast made us, and in Thy love wouldst make us perfect, we humbly confess that we have not loved Thee with all our heart and soul and mind and strength.*

The Calvin Shelds family of Knoll Park Lane went to San Francisco and left their cocker spaniel, Floppsie, to be fed by a neighbor, Robert Ogden. It was Carroll Huscher, though, not Ogden, who found the dog convulsing, obviously poisoned. It was Carroll Huscher who rushed the dog to the veterinarian.

When Mrs. Shelds came home and reported the incident to the Fallbrook Enterprise, she said that the poisoning had been deliberate, though she didn't point her finger at anyone in particular. Dr. Miller argued, just as cryptically, that such cases are usually accidental, "unless several cases of poisoning occur in the same neighborhood."

Floppsie recovered and came home the next day, in time for his story to be included in the same edition of the paper that told locals about Gladys Huscher's insanity plea and the appointment of two psychiatrists.

On May 16, Dr. G.W. Shannon, a female psychiatrist employed by Patton Hospital, introduced herself to Gladys Huscher. She asked questions about the past. She nodded and she made extensive notes.

In her letter to the Honorable John A. Hewicker, a judge known as "Hanging John," Dr. Shannon complained that she had spent two hours and twenty minutes with Gladys on May 16, 1957.

"The examination was unduly long," Dr. Shannon wrote, "because of the defendant's insistence on giving minute details and recounting events, which, although not directly connected with the criminal offense, served (she thought) to fill in the background of her marital disharmony. She also recounted at great length her many physical symptoms and her own sterling characteristics."

While it seems odd to fault a defendant for giving "minute details" about events that led to a murder and could lead to her own execution, Dr. Shannon's description of Gladys makes it clear how flimsy she found Gladys's arguments in her own defense.

"Mrs. Huscher is a rather short, stockily-built, middle-aged woman," Shannon wrote, "who related well but was self-centered and opinionated. She was obviously attempting to put herself in a good light and recounted that she, for many years, was the sole support of the family. There is a marked tendency to belittle her husband in his efforts and, by contrast, to point up her own character of hardworking, self-sacrificing, devoted wife and mother, who, in spite of poor health, maintained the family against all these terrible difficulties."

Dr. Shannon then proceeded, in great detail, to recount what Gladys told her about Carroll's infidelity. She quoted Gladys extensively and recorded her own reactions to what Gladys said.

"In a not too convincing way," Dr. Shannon wrote, "she stated that she accepted some responsibility for her husband's attitude and interest in another woman." When Gladys told Dr. Shannon about checking Carroll's odometer and learning where he had really parked his car, Dr. Shannon described Gladys as "smug." When Gladys told Dr. Shannon about the Valentine's Day visit, at which Carroll brought a valentine for both Judy and his wife, Dr. Shannon observed that "the defendant caused quite a scene, refused the Valentine in such a way that Judy became extremely upset and said, 'Why are you so mean to my daddy?'"

Gladys also described her own illnesses and ailments in great detail, but Dr. Shannon was unmoved. "Three years ago I had arthritis so bad that they had to dress and undress me," Gladys told her, and Dr. Shannon noted, "While saying this, [Gladys] smiled and assumed a martyr-like expression."

Dr. Shannon even pointed out discrepancies in Gladys's remarks. She told Gladys that despite claiming to have told no one about her difficulties with Carroll, "in the course of her conversation with me she had mentioned about six people with whom she had discussed the problem."

Gladys continued, nevertheless, to talk. She told Dr. Shannon about the weekend of Judy's death, relating her feelings of despair and weariness. She described the steps she took prior to sedating herself — how she gathered up her money, mailed it to her mother, and drove back home. Gladys said that she recalled mixing the strychnine, going to Judy's room, and spilling the liquid on the bed.

"She was asleep," Gladys told Dr. Shannon. "I remember spilling it. She swallowed it."

Dr. Shannon asked if Judy made any noise, and Gladys said that Judy did not cry out.

"[Gladys] does not remember how long she stayed with [Judy]," Dr. Shannon reported. "She does not remember how many sleeping pills she, herself, ingested."

Gladys did, however, recall writing the note to Dean, and

Gladys "insisted" that she wrote it before taking one-quarter of a bottle of belladonna and an unknown quantity of sleeping pills. Gladys added that she left the note in the bedroom, not the dining room, and that the next thing she remembered was waking up in the hospital on Tuesday.

It was to Dr. Shannon that Gladys confessed the same motive she had confessed to Deputy Majors: an unwillingness to give Judy to her husband's mistress.

"Two bottles of strychnine were in the garage," Gladys told Dr. Shannon. "I brought them to the sink and mixed them with something from the cupboard. I just couldn't see Judy going to the other woman. I couldn't stand her going to live with a person living in deceit." Gladys also told Dr. Shannon, confusingly, "I stirred up the strychnine for myself."

After hearing two hours and twenty minutes of self-justification and incrimination, Dr. Shannon wrote a scathing assessment of the woman Judge Joe Schell had chosen as Judy's mother.

First, in the midst of relating what Gladys had told her about Judy's death, Shannon interjected: "She shows remarkably little emotional affect when talking about the death of the girl, although she verbalizes that she loved her dearly. I get the distinct impression of this woman being a self-centered, planning, scheming, cold, hostile person, who must have displayed, for at least 18 years, many neurotic symptoms."

For at least 18 years. That would be six years before Judy's birth and four years prior to the moment when Judge Schell decided Gladys Huscher would be the best mother for Judith Ann.

In the formal conclusion to her report, Dr. Shannon wrote: "The defendant gave a clear, concise, and detailed description of her past life and of all the events which led to the attempted suicide and death of her adopted daughter. Obviously, she was in good contact with her surroundings and knew the nature of the actions and their consequences. We have only her own statement of her intention of using the strychnine for herself. It is evident that she had felt resentment about the child's devotion to her father and her growing fondness for her 'to-be-stepmother.'

"The acts were those of a frustrated woman, who was going to punish the man she claims to love. Her whole statement reveals a self-interested, neurotic woman who could not stand frustrations.

"It is my opinion that Gladys Bowes Teeple Huscher is sane and was sane at the time of the commission of her acts."

Dr. Shannon agreed with the district attorney, who charged that Gladys did "willfully, unlawfully, and with malice aforethought, kill and murder one Judith Ann Huscher, a human being." Dr. Shannon signed the letter that same afternoon and mailed it to Hanging John.

HOT AS A HARE

A week later, another psychiatrist came to call on Gladys Huscher. Dr. John Robuck spent just over an hour with Gladys Huscher on May 23, 1957 — about half as much time as Dr. Shannon spent. Perhaps Gladys had sensed Dr. Shannon's impatience with her lengthy explanations, so she vowed to shorten them. Perhaps Gladys elicited less hostility in a male examiner, or perhaps she simply went into less detail because she had told the full story a week before. Although Dr. Robuck's reaction to Gladys was much milder than Dr. Shannon's, he did feel that Gladys's way of talking about her daughter's murder was not quite normal.

"Mrs. Huscher presented herself to me as a 55-year-old woman of short stature who was neatly dressed and who appeared to be fully aware of her surroundings and to understand the purpose of my visit. She chatted rather amiably about herself and the subjects under discussion, crying briefly once when she mentioned her daughter. I was impressed with the rather inappropriateness of her feeling tone or affect throughout the interview and, in general, did not feel that she was normal in this respect. She was well-oriented in all spheres, showed no defects of memory or intellection (other than those to be described later), and gave no evidence suggesting the presence of hallucinations or delusions."

Gladys seems, during this rather amiable chat, to have told Dr.

Robuck a very different story about Judy's death.

"On the day of the daughter's death, Mrs. Huscher stated that she carried out a not unusual routine until her daughter had gone to bed at which point she finally determined that she was going to commit suicide. She gathered several containers of medication that had accumulated about the house and took about fifty tablets of belladonna (strength unknown). Her memory is hazy for events thereafter but she does recall thinking, 'Judy will find my body,' and being very concerned about the probable shock of this to her daughter. She believes, from what she has been told about the circumstances, that she then probably obtained some strychnine from the garage, where it had been used to kill rodents, and administered some to her daughter in order to insure her against the prospect of finding her mother dead. Her next clear recollection is of awaking in a hospital bed, with her sister at her side, some two or three days later."

In this version of events, Gladys portrays herself as someone who is merely confused. She is the Gladys Huscher who asked a fellow teacher, "What is it they say I have done?" and who makes a psychotic but slightly more sympathetic error of judgment — thinking that strychnine would protect her daughter from the trauma of finding her mother's dead body. Gladys did not tell Dr. Robuck what she told Dr. Shannon: that she remembered fetching the strychnine from the garage and mixing it with cocoa and spilling it on Judy's bed. She did not tell him that she abhorred the idea of giving Judy to a person living in deceit. She told him, instead, that she had inferred, from what other people said, that she had gone to the garage and gotten the poison. If Gladys did not remember poisoning Judy, then how could she have planned her death?

Although Gladys had told Deputy Majors that she didn't know whether she took "sleeping pills" before or after mixing the strychnine, Gladys clearly told Dr. Robuck that she took the pills first and that the pills were belladonna. Gladys's urine had tested "strongly positive" for barbiturates (Seconal is a barbiturate) and negative for strychnine, but no test, apparently, was done for belladonna, and Dr. Robuck didn't seem to be aware of the test results. Believing that Gladys was both drugged and confused, and believing that he knew what drug she had taken, Dr. Robuck came to a different conclusion about Gladys's guilt.

"It would be my opinion," he wrote, "that Mrs. Huscher was probably psychotic at least during the evening that preceded her daughter's death. Diagnostically, this would fall in the category of Psychotic Depressive Reaction and be the result of the emotional stress she had been experiencing in the dissolution of her marriage. It also seems probable that a dosage of fifty tablets of belladonna in any size likely to be prescribed by a physician would also produce a psychotic state in a relatively short time."

Mad as a hatter, blind as a bat, red as a beet, hot as a hare, dry as a bone.

"Since the exact time span between her ingestion of the belladonna and the act toward her daughter is not known, it seems very possible that a drug-induced psychosis was also a factor in her behavior. At the time of my examination, I found the aforementioned inappropriateness of affect as the chief deviation from normal in Mrs. Huscher. I did not feel that it was of such a degree that I would classify her as psychotic at that time although a more comprehensive examination consisting of observation by trained personnel over several days might demonstrate the current presence of psychosis."

In Fallbrook, the talk was mostly of the rain. If you didn't count May of 1955, it was the wettest year on record. Olallie berries at Rancho Lem-O-Lall-ee began to darken and plump up. Girls bought dresses for the junior-senior prom, and Queen Judy Diamond prepared to wave from her float as the Pioneer Days parade moved slowly down Main Street.

TRIAL

In June, the weather turned stifling. Temperatures soared to 100, and kids stood dumbstruck in the fields of Rancho Lem-O-Lall-ee, their fingers stained with olallieberry juice. Jimmy Armstrong, 13-year-old son of Mr. and Mrs. P.C. Armstrong, killed a rattler with a hoe. He said he intended to take the rattles off, skin the snake, and hang the skin in his bedroom.

Future Homemakers of America held their installation dinner at the new Fallbrook High School. The Reverend Stanley Smith gave a speech on aiming for the future, and gifts that would have gone to Gladys Huscher were given to her sweet young replacement, Margaret Slate, mother of an 11-month-old daughter, Barbara Faye.

Thirty prospective jurors assembled in the San Diego Courthouse on Monday, June 17. Claude Brown had not yet decided whether to seek the death penalty for Gladys, so he prepared to question the jurors on their attitudes toward capital punishment, then make his decision after he heard Mrs. Huscher's testimony. The prosecution's case was that Gladys poisoned Judy as an act of revenge — that she did it to hurt Carroll.

Eddie Langford told reporters it was practically a certainty that Mrs. Huscher would take the stand and that she would testify that she did not remember poisoning the child. She would refute her confession to Deputy Majors. Langford then went a step beyond what Gladys had told Dr. Robuck. He imagined a Gladys Huscher who never carried the strychnine into Judy's room and spooned it into her sleeping daughter's mouth.

"It's probable Mrs. Huscher intended to take the poison herself after the sleeping tablets," Langford said. "The child could have picked it up and drunk it." What Langford does not address in this theory is the presence of the spoon. If you wake up and wander into the kitchen, smell hot chocolate, see it sitting in a cup and drink it, would you use a spoon? What was a spoon doing in her bed?

Oddly, the defense and the prosecution said they would stipulate that Judy died of poisoning. "This will eliminate the necessity of bringing much unpleasant medical testimony and evidence before the jury," said the *San Diego Union*.

That meant the jury would never have to hear the coroner describe tetanic convulsions. The jury would never have to imagine the violent extension of her arms and legs, the terror that a poisoning victim feels as she waits for the next spasm. The tiny segments of Judy's organs, removed by the autopsy surgeon and sent to Thompson's medical laboratory, had done all the speaking they were going to do on her behalf: she was poisoned, sure enough. Perhaps Claude Brown intended to arouse the jurors' outrage by some other means.

On Monday, the hottest June 17th on record, 30 veniremen and women were questioned about their views on the death penalty. Brown asked prospective jurors if they had scruples about capital punishment and if they believed that a person who attempted suicide or killed another human being was necessarily insane. Upon hearing their responses, Brown eliminated twelve people, and the judge excused four who said that they saw the death penalty as the only suitable punishment for a convicted murderer. Langford eliminated four more. With sufficient time left to start the trial that same afternoon, the judge and the attorneys had agreed on eight women and four men.

Gladys's niece, Elizabeth, does not remember attending the trial. It was early summer, so she wouldn't have been teaching, but she had two boys to take care of. Elizabeth was her mother's source of transportation, so Madalene probably didn't attend either. If Ruth attended, she did so under strange conditions. Ruth Teeple Reid, a music teacher, an upstanding member of the Altrusa women's club, which dedicated itself to the assistance of abused women and children, would have been sitting in the courtroom as her sister refuted the confession she, Ruth, had heard first and had reported to the police.

One person did make the effort to attend the trial in spite of how long it took to drive from Fallbrook to San Diego in those days. Mrs. Morris, Judy's foster mother, drove an hour and a half each way to see what explanation would be offered, what justice might be done.

On that unpleasantly warm June afternoon, with temperatures downtown in the mid-90s, Mrs. Morris saw Gladys sitting beside her attorneys, Chuck and Eddie. She saw Claude Brown call the first witness for the prosecution: Judy's father, Carroll Huscher.

Huscher told the story that was bound to affect everyone in the room, the story of a father coming to his house and discovering his child, dead, in her room. He said he and Gladys had been estranged for some time. He said he'd purchased the strychnine at his wife's request.

Then Josephine Kelsey took the stand. She said that Gladys had been one of her dearest friends for 22 years. She identified the letter she'd received on the morning after Judy's death, and the letter became evidence for the jury to see.

Please forgive me. You tried hard to help me. I hope God will bless you in more ways than one. Gladys — I tried and J. you know I did, but I was not equal to those cocky smirky looks and conversations, and no understandings or chance to work it out. Always chaperoned in our home.

Although the letter would also be useful to Charles Provence — wasn't this the letter of a paranoid woman, a woman who was "off her rocker"? — the first sentence is certainly useful to the prosecution. A plea for forgiveness suggests that Gladys planned to do something hard to forgive and that she was planning it as early as Friday, March 29.

When Eddie Langford cross-examined Kelsey, he asked if she had received a phone call from Gladys Huscher.

Kelsey said she had. She had talked to Mrs. Huscher by telephone on Saturday, March 30.

"Did she appear to be disturbed?" Langford asked.

"Objection," Brown said, and Judge Glen agreed, forbidding further questions in this line.

The next witness was Deputy Majors. He had time only to identify a few exhibits and pictures before Judge Glen recessed the trial. In the morning, Deputy Majors would come back to relate what he'd heard in Tiny's hospital.

Whatever Majors said on that Tuesday morning, which was as hot as the morning before, the jurors found it convincing. They did not doubt his ability to remember Mrs. Huscher saying, "I did it so the other woman wouldn't be able to have her if I died." When Gladys took the stand and denied what Majors had said about her confession, they did not believe her. In his closing arguments, Claude Brown asked the jury to "consider the fact that Judy, an innocent child, is dead. It is reasonable to suppose it was done vindictively."

The jurors agreed with him. They decided, after just two and a half days of testimony and 85 minutes of deliberation, during three days of record-breaking heat, that Gladys Huscher was guilty of first-degree murder — that the circumstances attending the killing showed what the jury instructions called "an abandoned and malignant heart." They did not recommend her execution, but they said she should spend the rest of her life in prison.

"Mrs. Huscher, a gray-haired teacher of home economics in Fallbrook High School for 15 years," the *San Diego Union* reported on the front page, "heard the verdict calmly. It was some minutes before she started to weep."

THE SANITY HEARING

The heat wave was over, but the trial was not. In 1957, a murder trial such as Mrs. Huscher's was conducted in two parts. First the jury would decide if the defendant was guilty or not guilty. Then, if they found the defendant guilty, they would hear testimony regarding her sanity. If they found her sane on March 31, Judge Glen would set a date to hear motions for a new trial and formal sentencing. A sane Gladys Huscher would face an average of 11 years in prison before parole.

If, however, they found she was insane that night, the life sentence would be set aside. Gladys Huscher would be committed to a state mental hospital for at least one year.

In the 1950s, statisticians calculated that one family in three would admit a family member to a mental institution. By 1959, some 800,000 Americans were in mental hospitals, and few of them would ever win release. In 1955, only 4700 psychiatrists were licensed to practice in the United States, and only 500 new psychiatrists joined them each year. Despite the impressive amount of money spent during this decade on medical research, little of it went to mental health. "As a result," wrote Bruccoli and Layman in *American Decades: 1950–1959,* "many mental institutions became overcrowded warehouses where tormented people waited to die."

Mrs. Huscher's jury took a short recess and Provence met with the Fallbrook residents he'd called to testify. "I won't have a chance to meet with you again before you go on the stand this afternoon," he told them, "but do this for me. You know what we need, so write out a list of questions for each of you that will bring out the best you have on the subject."

Gladys Huscher's fellow teachers and friends had heard the sentence: *murder in the first degree and life in prison.* They did what Provence asked. They wrote questions that would elicit their best anecdotes about insane behavior.

"I had to modify their questions slightly, to avoid objections," Provence wrote. "The result was one of the easiest and most effective examinations of witnesses I had ever done."

When the recess was over, Provence stood before the jury and said the defense would prove, through the testimony of Gladys Huscher's friends and relatives, that Mrs. Huscher was a manic-depressive. Manic depression is not temporary insanity. It doesn't descend, in a flash, after you've taken too many pills or received a hard blow to the heart, and it doesn't disappear afterwards. But manic-depressive is the diagnosis Provence chose.

He called to the stand four women who had known Gladys for at least 22 years, who had associated with her since Gladys came to Fallbrook High. They all testified that Gladys "must have been insane" on March 31.

Mrs. Owens testified that Gladys was fine on Saturday, the 30th, but insane by Sunday, the 31st. Mrs. Kelsey said, "If she had been sane she couldn't have committed the deed."

Mrs. Martha Scott, a former Fallbrook resident who had moved to La Mesa, said Gladys "could not have been sane at the time if I'm to take the jury's opinion that she was guilty." Mrs. Scott believed, as did the Vixes, that her guilt was in some doubt.

Claude Brown asked Mrs. Scott when she'd last seen Gladys. Mrs. Scott said she'd seen her on February 22.

"Did you have an opinion then that she didn't know the

difference between right and wrong?" Brown asked.

"Well, hardly," said Mrs. Scott.

Ruby Aaberg said that she believed Gladys had been mentally ill since 1939 — for 18 years, just as Dr. Shannon theorized. Gladys had threatened to jump off a bridge because of her troubles with Dean, but Ruby said she hadn't taken her seriously.

When it was the prosecution's turn to question Ruby, Claude Brown asked about Gladys's return to work after her breakdown in 1939. "But she went back to teaching?" he asked.

"She sure did," Mrs. Aaberg said. "She was a good teacher."

Brown asked Aaberg, Owens, Scott, and Kelsey if they believed Judy was in danger. No, they said. No.

Judge Glen listened to these witnesses and said, in front of the jury, "Mr. Provence, don't you think you have produced enough witnesses to support your contentions?"

"Yes, your honor," Provence said, "we have many more, but I will call only one or two more after this."

On Thursday, June 20, it was time for the experts to speak. Three psychiatrists were called to testify about Gladys's mental state that night: Dr. Robuck, Dr. Shannon, and Dr. Albin F. Meyer. Robuck said he believed Mrs. Huscher to be a psychotic depressive. Dr. Meyer described her as a "seriously disturbed, emotionally ill person." Perhaps because Dr. Shannon was the assistant superintendent of Patton State Hospital, she was accorded the most space in the newspaper account of Thursday's testimony. She said she had received the impression, during her examination of Gladys, that Mrs. Huscher had "an unspoken hostility toward the girl because she was a daddy's girl and because she was not brilliant in school."

Carroll Huscher, called to testify yet again, said, "My wife's first love was her school, her second was her mother, her third was myself, and her fourth was Judy."

Ruth Reid and Madalene Sage were present for this part of the trial and they testified their sister had threatened to kill herself.

They said that Gladys, their sister, was insane.

The jurors considered this in light of what they had been told in the jury instructions: "You must determine the condition of her mind at the precise time of the criminal conduct of which she has been found guilty. Although you may consider evidence of her mental state before and after that time, such evidence is to be considered only for the purpose of throwing light upon her mental condition as it was when the offense was committed."

Was she insane, meaning in such a "diseased and deranged condition of the mental faculties as to render her incapable of knowing the nature and quality of her act"? Did she "know and understand that it was a violation of the rights of another, and in itself wrong"?

"Temporary insanity as a defense to crime," they were told, "is as fully recognized by law as is insanity of long duration." Temporary insanity was a defense, but moral insanity was not.

"Moral insanity, in itself, is not a bar to responsibility for criminal acts; hence, howsoever perverted, if at all, the feelings, conscience, affections, and sentiments of a person may be, unless the intellectual faculties and reasoning powers are so affected by mental disease as to render him incapable of distinguishing between right and wrong…he is responsible to the law for his criminal acts."

In Dr. Shannon's opinion, Gladys was morally insane: her feelings, conscience, affections, and sentiments were perverted. She was a "cold-blooded person who deliberately planned to do as much harm as she could." According to this reasoning, which was also the theory of the prosecution, Gladys blamed her daughter for being a poor student and for being so easily and utterly loved by the man who had stopped loving her. She also committed the moral outrage of being a woman who loved her work more, as Carroll testified, than she loved her daughter.

To Dr. Meyer and Dr. Robuck, however, and to Gladys's friends and relatives, Gladys was in a less culpable state. She could not help it.

RESOLVE

San Diego Bay was a cool blue stripe at the west end of Broadway on Friday, June 21. The jurors left the fresh, summer-bright world, with its white sails and glinting water, for the room where they wondered which definition of insanity applied to a woman who had walked into her daughter's room and spooned chocolate poison into her trusting mouth. The foreman, Nolan Wright, asked Judge Glen to read portions of the testimony back. Wright told the judge he and the other jurors found the psychiatrists' testimony vague and contradictory.

"It's your job to resolve the conflicts," Glen told them.

It was the longest day of the year, the first day of summer. Inside the room, the jurors talked and talked. The bay flickered beyond the window, rocked the boats in the harbor, and explained nothing. As afternoon became evening, cars moved slowly up and down Broadway, red lights following white lights following red, the arrivals and departures of people on holiday, people who were free to go. They talked through dinner, past the hours of seven, eight, and nine. The bay was black when they made their decision: Gladys Huscher was temporarily but not morally insane when she walked into her daughter's room with a cup of poisoned chocolate, picked up the spoon, looked down at her sleeping child, and brought the sweet smell of chocolate close to Judy's face.

They ruled that she could not help it.

"Thus Mrs. Huscher escapes the life sentence imposed Wednesday by the same jury," the *Union* reporter wrote. "The county psychiatrist now will examine her and if he determines Mrs. Huscher now is sane, she will go free. If he finds that she is insane, she faces commitment to Patton State Hospital."

A strange loosening had occurred between Wednesday and Friday. On Wednesday, Gladys Huscher had been told she would spend the rest of her life in prison. Now she didn't have to go. She might go to the lunatic asylum, the funny farm, the loony bin, the nuthouse, or she might, just might, walk blinking and well-shod into the general world, a world where, to be sure, she had no job, no town, no husband, and no daughter, but one where she would nevertheless be free to walk, drive, shop, cook, sew, and eat dinner on a well-ironed tablecloth.

Two more psychiatrists came to see her, different ones this time. Dr. C.E. Lengyel and Dr. W.G. Wiegand asked her questions, studied her face, her movements, her reactions to this and that. Whether they asked Gladys Huscher about Judy's death or her husband, they didn't say.

"She presents the overt picture of an affable, sociably inclined individual…" they observed. "She has exhibited no evidence of any emotional or mental disorder…she does not entertain any bizarre trends."

She was not, in their opinion, manic-depressive. She had suffered a psychotic depressive reaction, and it was over now.

Provence was uneasy. He didn't entirely agree with Lengyel and Wiegand. "The rule, then, was that if a defendant was found not guilty by reason of insanity, the judge could, nevertheless, if he thought she was dangerously insane, order her detained for one year for observation and treatment."

Provence didn't think she was dangerous, but he thought she was "nuts a good part of the time and that she would go to pieces as soon as she was released and have to have medical treatment."

Provence suggested to Langford that they tell the judge to detain her.

"Hell, no," Langford said. "Let's walk her out onto the street."

A different judge, the Honorable L.N. Turrentine, ordered the jail wardens to release Gladys Huscher on June 28. "The law compels it," he said.

Gladys's family was evidently surprised. "I don't know how Chuck got her off," Gladys's niece, Elizabeth, said 45 years later.

On Saturday morning, June 29, the headline "Mrs. Huscher Judged Sane, Wins Freedom" appeared on the front page of the *San Diego Union*, next to a photograph of Elmer David Vorce and his wife Wilma, at graveside ceremonies for their six-year-old daughter, Mallory Sue. As *Union* subscribers and summer tourists read about Gladys's future plans ("she will reside temporarily with relatives in Chula Vista"), they read, also, about Mr. Vorce, whose guilt and sorrow were more familiarly expressed.

"Elmer David Vorce, 32, sobbed uncontrollably yesterday at the funeral of his stepdaughter, Mallory Sue, 6, whom he is accused of beating to death. Vorce, a milkman, is charged with the fatal beating of Mallory Sue last Monday in his North Park apartment. Police said he admitted slapping the girl because she hadn't washed dishes properly. The girl died six hours later of a brain hemorrhage and a ruptured spleen."

Charles Provence told reporters that "efforts would be made" to persuade Gladys to enter the mental hospital of her own free will. He knew that people would be outraged at the verdict. "As usual, when a defendant otherwise obviously guilty is released by a defense of insanity, the public is very aggravated, and so was the Grand Jury that was in session at the time of our verdict."

Charles Provence's wife, Winifred, was a member of the grand jury, and Provence was a little surprised to read in the papers that his wife and the other jurors were investigating his defense of Mrs. Huscher.

"What's this?" he asked, but he wasn't especially concerned. "I wasn't worried at all," he wrote, "and after they learned a little about the law of insanity and the evidence in our case, they backed off fast."

It was June, almost July. The *Enterprise* still carried ads for "C" Huscher's Meats: round steak, ground beef, rolled roast, and wieners. "Buy Your Meat at "C" Huscher's Where You Save $$$$$$."

Rancho Lem-O-Lall-ee still invited pickers to select berries from its fields, and Safeway had a sale on Snow Star chocolate ice cream. High school students on holiday walked in the twilight to the ticket counter of the Mission Theater, brushing hands as they paid to see James Stewart play Lucky Lindy in *The Spirit of St. Louis*. Then they filled their lungs with sweet night air and walked home in the dark, passing house after house where the lamps and televisions were on, where the windows were open, where death had not lain behind a closed bedroom door on a girl's narrow bed.

TO PIECES

As Charles Provence had predicted, Gladys Huscher went to pieces after her release. She came apart, as he put it. For this she was hospitalized and given shock treatment.

Electroshock therapy was the preferred form of treatment for mental health patients in the '50s because it was cheap. It was thought particularly useful in treating depression, manic-depression, and involuntary melancholia. An electric current passed through Gladys Huscher's brain and induced convulsions not unlike those that Judy felt before she died. The convulsions could, in some cases, be so violent that patients broke bones pulling against the restraints, but if Gladys Huscher suffered in this way, her niece Elizabeth did not remember it. She didn't remember, at first, that Gladys had been in a hospital at all.

"A little glimmer comes. I may have heard about it," she said. "I haven't thought about it for a long time."

Gladys left the hospital without a job. She didn't have enough money to retire on and she wasn't old enough to begin collecting Social Security. She began to live under her maiden name, which nobody knew. It was Gladys Huscher who had been in all the papers, not Gladys Bowes Teeple.

"After she was released," Charles Provence wrote, "she would call me at home, at dinner time, too frequently. I would get mad and say, 'That woman is crazy,' and Winifred would say, 'Yes, Dear, she is. You proved that.' "

Gladys's niece did remember what her aunt did next. Gladys Teeple moved to Culver City, where she got a job as a saleswoman in a "very fancy dress shop" by the name of Quist's. "She knew style and she knew fabric and the whole thing. They were glad to get her," Elizabeth said. "Oh, they liked her." The Quist family even included Gladys in their family gatherings, such as Christmas.

It was a long drive to Culver City from Chula Vista, but Gladys's sisters and their children drove up to see Gladys every August, to celebrate her birthday.

On March 31, 1958, the first anniversary of Judy's death, Gladys's mother died. She had been living in Fredericka Manor, a community of bungalows, apartments, and hospital rooms that formed the Chula Vista Methodist home.

In 1959, Warren Sage, the brother-in-law who had persuaded Charles Provence to be Gladys's attorney, died there, too. Gladys kept selling clothes, suggesting outfits, remarking on the suitability of this color and that. In 1967, when she was finally old enough to collect Social Security, she said good-bye to the Quists and moved into Fredericka Manor herself, into a little house on Saylor Drive. She brought with her the silver monogrammed with a T, her mother's hand-painted china, and the jewelry, hats, suits, and dresses she'd bought with her discount at Quist's.

"She always was so well-dressed," Elizabeth said from her own apartment at Fredericka Manor. "A lady who eats at my table remembers my aunt. She had these gorgeous clothes and hats, and that's because she'd worked at Quist's."

In 1974, Gladys became ill and entered the Manor's hospital. "My husband took over her expenses after Gladys went in the hospital," Elizabeth said. "We went to the hospital to visit Gladys, and what she always wanted was hand lotion. She had a thing about hand lotion."

It was time to dispose of Gladys's things. For herself, Elizabeth kept a desk and the hand-painted Teeple family china. Elizabeth found a grandniece whose last name started with T and gave her the silver Gladys had kept since she was a young teacher in Oceanside. Elizabeth does not recall any mementos or photographs of Judy. She and her husband held a garage sale and sold the fashionable clothes from Quist's, the suits of a bygone era, the hats out of date, the brooches, earrings, pins, and chokers.

At 4:30 p.m., on December 7, 1974, Gladys Bowes Teeple died of heart failure. What remained of her after cremation was placed in a niche long occupied by the ashes of the person her former husband had said she loved most of all: her mother.

THE BEST THING

On August 7, 1957, the property department of the San Diego sheriff's office sent a memo to Deputy Majors, requesting advice about the evidence collected at the Huscher house: *Box containing two sheets, a pillowcase, bedpad, and a towel. Box containing four jars. Box containing victim's clothing: Judith Ann Huscher.*

When the memo reached Deputy Majors, he wrote, "Please inform and request Mr. Dean Huscher of Fallbrook, Oak Knoll Lane, to pick up articles except the jars. Throw them away." Two days later, Carroll Huscher drove to San Diego to collect those terrible boxes and to sign his name beside a statement that he was the legal owner of two spoons, two cups, one towel, one saucepan, one roll of toilet paper, and the pajamas his daughter put on before she died.

Bette, meanwhile, was preparing to leave Fallbrook for Northern California. The strawberry cooperative once managed, in part, by Carroll Huscher had failed, and local farmers had lost money. The president of the co-op had subsequently committed suicide, and Bette's opinion of Mr. Huscher "changed from dislike to a deeper sense of dread."

In the fall, Bette transferred to the University of California at Berkeley. "I lived at the International House with a roommate. Sometime during my first year there, I received a call from Mr.

Huscher from downstairs. I asked my roommate to take it and give him an excuse for not talking to him. Simply, I did not want to have anything to do with him. After a week or so, he gave up."

Carroll may have found himself in Berkeley because he was, by then, a salesman based in Sacramento. His territory included the Rexall pharmacy on Mission and 16th Street in San Francisco, where he found himself drawn to one of the employees. He learned her name was Constance Martinez and that she had a daughter. "They married when I was ten years old," said the daughter, whose name is Linda, "and we moved to Sacramento."

What follows are excerpts from letters Linda Huscher wrote about her stepfather, whose name she took out of respect for him and what he had done for her and her family.

"My Dad was bowlegged," she wrote. "He liked cowboy hats and boots. He loved to laugh and he would clap his hands when he told a funny joke. He loved to tease. He would try to speak Spanish and roll his r's and we would laugh. He called us the 'tribe.'"

When told that rumors circulated in Fallbrook that Carroll Huscher was a womanizer and may have been abusive to both Judy and Gladys, Linda wrote:

"My mother was born in Mexico, one of six children. She has two sisters and three brothers (only one surviving). Her mother raised all of them by herself. They were very poor. My grandmother, though illiterate, felt education was the only way her children would do better. The oldest daughter went to work and put my mother and the others through school. My mother graduated from college and became a teacher. English was her major and she speaks it fluently. The family was very united and helped each other. My mother married when she was 31 and I was born in 1952 (she was 32). I was born in San Antonio, Texas, while she was on a visit to my aunt.

"A few days after my birth she went back to Mexico. My biological father left when I was born and refused to help in any way. She and I went to live alongside the river in Piedras Negras (a border town on the other side of Eagle Pass, Texas). We lived in a one-room shack with a dirt floor, no windows, no running water, and no electricity until my mother received her papers to cross into the United States. We then moved in with my aunt (her sister). From there we went to live in San Francisco with her other sister, her husband and four kids. I was five years old. My mother found a job at the Rexall Pharmacy on Mission and 16th Street," where Carroll Huscher came to call.

In 1962, Constance and Linda joined Carroll in Sacramento. If Carroll had been in the habit of abusing a wife and daughter, he had now created a situation very like the one he had lost, far away from anyone who knew his past.

Linda was not particularly happy to have Carroll for a father at first. "I was resentful that this man was taking me away from my cousins and the only secure place I had known. When you describe Judy, it feels like you're describing me when I was that age. I was [un]attractive, socially inadequate, fearful and angry. It amazes me that my father would take such a risk again. I can only imagine he truly loved us."

Linda saw no abuse of her mother, and Carroll didn't try to hide his past from them, or even to blame Gladys.

"I have always thought that Gladys was a poor desperate soul. My father never spoke a harsh word against Gladys and he most definitely never said anything negative about Judy. That he loved Judy dearly was very clear. In fact, he was the kind of man who would not gossip, or speak harshly to anyone. He never raised his voice or a hand against my mother or me. My mother has always said that he was a gentle man and he treated her like she was made out of glass — fragile. And, there was also never any indication that he was not loyal to his marriage vows."

She doesn't think her mother would have accepted a marriage like that.

"My mother is a very independent, assertive, courageous

woman. She speaks her mind and stands up for her rights. I've heard stories about her chasing a chicken thief, organizing a group of men to stop trucks going to feed the rich and bypassing the poor people when our town in Mexico suffered a flood. I've seen her confront injustice and defend those who she felt needed defending. She is loved and respected by her neighbors and friends. She is not a person who would let anyone raise a hand against her or anyone she loved. She would never tolerate infidelity or disrespect."

After Carroll married Constance, he continued to visit his sisters in Fallbrook. He kept Judy's photograph over his dresser. He kept Judy's clothes too, and a box of her possessions, the little figurines of animals, tiny vases, souvenir spoons from Chicago, San Francisco, Palm Springs, and Ireland. He kept the Mickey Mouse ceramic bowl with the inscription that says "Hello Judy." He kept a miniature bride.

"Why did he leave Fallbrook? My guess is that the memories were too painful. If we were watching TV and there was a scene with a woman or child screaming, he would close his eyes as tight as he could, cover his ears with his hands, trying to block out the sound, and he would leave the room crying. He told me once that he imagined that Judy must have died in a great deal of pain.

"I've always suspected he left a prosperous business in Fallbrook. However, he never said one way or the other and he never seemed to regret the decision. I suspect that the day Judy died, he really lost everything that mattered to him.

"Our life was comfortable; one I would describe as middle-class to lower middle-class. We never lacked for the essentials, and he was not frivolous with money."

He worked as a credit manager for a supermarket chain, then as a marketing consultant. "Once he retired, it was like he went downhill. He was a very social person, and he liked to be useful." He got sick in 1988, when he was 81 years old, and he died two weeks later.

"When he died, I was actually worried we would not have the funds for his burial; however, he managed to save a few thousand, which is amazing since he did not make a lot of money.

"I said to you that he was the best thing that ever happened to me. Let me explain. My only memory of my biological father was my mother asking him for money so that she could buy milk for me. He refused. My mother wrote him when I was 12 asking if she could send me so that I could get to know him. He said yes, but I would have to pay rent. You can imagine the baggage I was carrying when my dad married my mother. What story would I use to support the statement I made to you? The story of his life with me. He was always there for me. He loved me no matter what I did or what I said. He never judged me. He showed me unconditional love. He showed me kindness. He showed me integrity. He gave me respect. He gave me a life."

Linda Huscher wrote these letters in spite of her doubts about what her father would have wanted. He was a private man, she said.

"For a few days I wondered whether I actually needed to defend him or set the record straight. Knowing him, he would say, 'Let people think and say what they want to; it's no business of theirs.'"

ETERNAL HILLS

Judy Huscher's grave is in Oceanside, in a cemetery called Eternal
Hills. You can hear the train from there and the rush of cars. The
Court of the Cross Urn Garden, where her ashes were buried
more than 50 years ago, is a green slope with wide prospects. Small
rectangular stones lie flat on the ground. The grass tries to cover
them and is mown on Wednesdays. Some stones are so completely
buried by clipped grass that you have to sweep them with your hand
to read the names. They are old people, by and large, her neighbors.
Only "Baby Girl" Powroznik died younger than she. Judy's stone,
which says simply "Judy Huscher, 1945–1957," sits between Hank
Decking and an oleander tree, whose long, poisonous leaves make
flickering shadows on her name. The heavy roseate blooms drop
down on her stone and wither, leaving dark blottings of themselves,
a curled hieroglyphic that will wash away, little by little, when the
sprinklers come on.

THE LAST MEETING

OF THE DOVE CLUB

A PIONEER FAMILY'S TRAGEDY

INTRODUCTION

This history of the Ed Fletcher family in San Diego was originally published in the San Diego *Reader* on July 17, 1997. It relies on the complete court transcript of the murder trial of Ed Fletcher III, newspaper articles, a large archive of material relating to the Fletcher family held by the San Diego Historical Society, Colonel Ed Fletcher's memoir, and taped, transcribed interviews with the witnesses who are quoted in the story.

THOSE WHO WOULD DO ME HARM

On the eve of the annual dove hunt in Borrego Springs, California, a full moon was rising over 600,000 acres of desert. Eric and Beatrice Fletcher walked in the August heat toward a watering hole for doves, killing time until someone came home and unlocked the house where they were supposed to have dinner. There was no hurry, really, because once the house was unlocked, things would have to be said that no one wanted to say and no one wanted to hear.

They'd left their two children at home in El Cajon and driven for more than an hour and a half. The hunt was a tradition Eric had with his father, but his father was drinking too much, and so was his mother, and Eric's brother Kent was threatening people in all kinds of ways. It was the sort of family trouble you'd walk thousands of miles to get away from if you could.

The Anza-Borrego Desert is the largest state park in California, and Borrego Springs lies in the center of all that heat and solitude. It's home to just 2,000 people, many of them winter residents, so when Eric and Beatrice reached the mudhole just before sunset, they would have been pleasantly, gratefully alone. Mourning doves at the edge of the water made that curious peeping sound, fluttered, and rose. So many doves were taking flight that Eric looked down at his watch to take note: 7:14. A good time to hunt tomorrow.

When Eric looked back at the house where he and his two brothers had grown up together, he could see that a car had returned. His mother was in her bedroom asleep because she'd had too much to drink, though she didn't normally do that when Eric and Beatrice were expected. His father, who had been drinking all day, must now be home from the meeting of the dove club with his friends Walter and Carrlene.

Eric and Beatrice walked back toward the house: 10 yards, 20 yards, 30. The sky was still pink in the west. They were halfway home when, in all that silence, they heard the explosion of a fired gun. A woman screamed. The gun was racked and fired again. Eric told his wife to run and hide while he went up to the house alone.

Eric would testify in court that he ran to the glass wall that surrounds the pool. Through the transparent wall and the family room window, he could see his father holding a shotgun. He heard his father say, "I'm going to get that son of a bitch."

Eric walked carefully around the perimeter of the house, trying not to be seen, trying to figure out who was shooting. He knew that Walter and Carrlene Harper were in the house. The Harpers, besides coming down for dinner, had planned to stay the night, so they might have gone to their bedroom, where they would now be hiding in fear. Eric tapped on the window of that room, but no one answered. He made another careful circuit of the house and saw that a light was on in the master bedroom.

From beneath his parents' bedroom window, he heard his mother say, "Oh, my God, honey. You shot the kids."

This was a terrifying thing to hear, but it made no sense. Eric was one of their kids, and he hadn't been shot. Beatrice had run to hide in the airplane hangar south of Stinson Road. No other "kids" were home, unless it was his brother Kent, who had come by earlier to ask for money. Eric ran around the garage and dared to open the front door. From the hallway, he could hear his parents talking. They were still in the master bedroom, so he thought maybe he could walk into the kitchen, see what had happened, and then get safely out of the way.

He opened another door and saw what appeared to be legs on the kitchen floor. He took two more steps and saw that it was Walter and Carrlene Harper lying face up beside the oven, the refrigerator, and the cupboards that he knew so well. Their eyes were open but they saw nothing, and there was blood — so much blood — on the wall.

This night that would last for years and years was just beginning. The police, the lawyers, the subpoena, the trial in which Eric would have to be the key witness against his father, the TV cameras, the newspaper reporters, all that was yet to come. Outside in the desert, where his wife crouched down in the bushes beside an airplane hangar, waiting for him, it was beginning to get dark.

THE COLONEL

Good name in man and woman, dear my lord
Is the immediate jewel of their souls.
— Iago in *Othello* III.ii

The man pacing with the shotgun at the Borrego Air Ranch was Ed Fletcher III. He had always been proud of his name, and with good reason. He wasn't just a full-blooded third-generation Fletcher, but Ed Fletcher. The whole name had been handed down like a crown to his father, and then to him.

In reports about his arrest and trial, Ed Fletcher III would be called a scion of the Fletcher dynasty. His grandfather, the first Ed Fletcher, had done everything required of American monarchs: he rose from poverty, he acquired land, he became a millionaire, he held public office, and he fathered ten heirs. He liked to be called the Colonel, a title he'd earned in the state militia. When he dictated his memoirs, the Colonel traced his ancestors back to William the Conqueror's men and a Flechere who owned the Castle of Chillon. On a trip to Europe, he went to Lake Geneva, visited the castle, bought an etching of it, and hung it on his wall. He found the Fletcher coat of arms and made it the first illustration in his memoir. "Fletcher of Salton," it reads, "DIEU POUR NOUS." His son, Ed Fletcher, Jr., would later find that Fletcher of Salton was not their ancestor, that the Fletchers were actually descended from Gypsies who manufactured arrows, and that the family motto was not *Dieu pour nous*, but *Nec querere nec apernere honorem* ("Neither to seek nor to despise honor"), but that was nothing be ashamed of. For nearly a hundred years, the name Ed Fletcher received little else but honor in San Diego.

Mary and Ed Fletcher Sr., 50th wedding anniversary

Colonel Ed Fletcher was born on New Year's Eve, 1872, in Littleton, Massachusetts to the wife of a man who already had four daughters and a problem with alcohol. Charles Fletcher had been a wealthy, successful man just seven years before Ed was born, but he had co-signed the note on his brother Sherman's mill, where lumber was processed and where all the neighbors ground their flour until the mill burned down. The mill was not insured, so when Sherman declared bankruptcy, Charles had to pay Sherman's debts. He lost his house. Next he put $500 down on a 118-acre farm inherited by his niece and worked off the property taxes by maintaining roads. Instead of farming, he drank applejack and played poker in the barn with his friends.

Charles's wife Anna, who looks in her hazy photograph like a Greek statue in a Victorian dress, gave birth to Susie, Bess, Mary, Belle, Edward, and Steve before she died. To Ed and Bessie she gave the precise mold of her face: the cut of her lips, the shape of her nose, the slope of her eyelids. Ed was four when she died, old enough to form two memories: his mother passing candy to him through a hole in the fence and his mother in a coffin. Years and years later, a Sunday school teacher in San Diego would tell him that Unitarians couldn't enter the Kingdom of Heaven. Ed would retort that his mother had been a Unitarian, and he was willing to go where she went.

Susie and Bess Fletcher, aged 14 and 12 when their mother died, went to work in a chocolate factory. Ed and Steve went bone hunting in the meadows, gathering the bones of dead cows and selling them to a factory that ground them for fertilizer. In his memoir, Ed would leave out the bone gathering, just as he would leave out his father's drinking and his own nervous breakdown. For his children and grandchildren he would recall blueberries, huckleberries, frog legs, butter crackers, and the fish he caught with the father who abandoned him.

In 1881, four years after Anna died, Charles Fletcher left his children and went to live in Florida. He put the four children who were too young to marry or live alone into three separate houses. Ed, eight, and his sister Belle, ten, went to a cousin's farm "to earn our board and clothes."

"I remember yet," Ed would say in his memoir, "with almost a shiver, my experience on the William Kimball farm." He slept in the attic with the rats. The Kimballs woke him at four every morning to milk 11 cows, and he milked the same 11 cows again each night.

After school, his job was to dig holes for the rocks he found in the pasture and bury them so the topsoil could be farmed. While he and his sister Belle worked for the Kimballs, their father sent gifts from Florida: a live alligator, a box of oranges, and a gold watch that Ed would keep in working order for more than 70 years.

Ed's schoolteacher was a single woman named Jessie Wood who lived with her parents on the back road to Littleton Depot. Ed told Miss Wood about the Kimball farm and she listened so sympathetically that one night he packed his clothes and walked to her house. He said he would never go back there — back to the Kimballs and the rats. Miss Wood and her parents took him in, but Ed's sister Belle stayed with the Kimballs.

"My life with the Woods was a happy one," Ed wrote, "and as long as I live, I shall keep them in memory." The memories he kept for 70 years, ticking like the gold watch in San Diego, are an elegy to ice. He stuck his tongue to a frozen horse bit. He boasted to a girl that he could jump a stone wall in a pair of skates, and when he landed, he broke through the ice on the other side. After making ice cream in a tub of salted ice, he mixed chicken feed with the same salty water and, to his horror, killed 50 chickens that belonged to the family that had taken him in. On winter days, he threw stones down on the ice above perch and pickerel, then caught the stunned fish with his hands. "It was black, clear ice," he recalled, "which would bend but not break." On that black and almost endless ice he went sliding from shore to shore.

When Ed was nearly 12, he went to live in Boston with his sister Bessie, who would lead him, in a few years, to San Diego. It was Bessie who worked for a magazine called the *Youth's Companion*, whose face was both severe and gentle, whose face was like Ed's and her mother's: the straight nose, the curved lips, the flat cheeks. In Boston, he sold newspapers on Saturday and Sunday nights, and Bessie found him work in the shipping department of a wholesale dry goods store. He worked 10 hours a day for $2.50 a week. Until he was 77 years old he would remember the day that Bessie sent him on a holiday trip to Cape Cod. The ticket cost her $1 (half a day's wages) and the straw hat with the red ribbon — the one that would blow off into the sea — cost her 75 cents. He vomited into the wind and soiled the ministers who sat beside him, and when somebody hollered "Whale!" he was too sick to look.

In 1887, Bessie married a man named Jarvis Doyle and moved to San Diego. She and Aunt Susie decided Ed was too young to stay in Boston alone, so they found a family named Taft in Ayer, Massachusetts, who would take care of him and send him to school if he would do chores and work in the garden. So Ed moved again, started attending the Broomfield School, and earned money when he could. He picked wild strawberries, huckleberries, and hickory nuts. He gathered pond lilies at Flannigan's Pond and sold them to passengers waiting at the depot. One evening on his way through the birch grove that stood between the Tafts' vegetable garden and the house, he heard a girl asking for help.

"Looking around," he wrote, "I saw that a girl had climbed a tree to swing the birches. She had not climbed high enough, the limb had bent over, she was caught by her panties and there she hung 10 or 12 feet from the ground, head down, and all I could see was fluffy white and arms and legs. I climbed the birch tree, which, with my added weight, brought the limb down to the ground."

Ed noticed that the lace on her panties was two inches wide, and Mary, who was embarrassed, refused to tell Ed her name. They didn't meet again until they both attended the same party and Ed, who was in charge of a 19th-century version of Truth or Dare, told Mary to kiss the fellow she loved best. She kissed Ed, and "I started going with her immediately."

On a summer day when Flannigan's Pond was blooming with pond lilies, they set out in a boat. Ed carried a muzzle-loading shotgun, which he aimed at a kingfisher and fired. Ed and Mary were both standing at the time, and the force of the blast threw them into the water. "When I climbed in the boat," Ed said, "it was half-filled with water, Mary was gone, and looking over the side I saw her splashing around among the lilies." He saved her, and they went steady through the fall and winter, skating at night on that black and flexible ice. The next summer, they pushed a boat into the same pond and caught a three-foot freshwater eel that nearly drowned them again. But Ed got Mary to shore and called it "another one of the experiences of life where everything comes out all right."

In 1889, Ed received a letter from his father in Florida in which his father threatened to put him out to work as an apprentice, so Ed wrote to his brother-in-law, Jarvis, in San Diego. Jarvis sent $20 to help Ed keep his independence and come to California.

Perhaps because he'd worked for wages since he was old enough to lug cow bones from the pasture, his memories of that defining moment are scattered with sums. Although his son would eventually correct the year that Ed Fletcher arrived in San Diego (not 1888 but 1889), it was the Colonel who recorded the precise amount, to the dime, that he had in his pocket when he stepped off the train ($6.10). He remembered that he deposited five of those dollars in the San Diego Trust & Savings Bank on the very first day of his arrival, September 3, and that it was there he met the man who would give him his first job.

The moment he stepped off the train and into that bank, Ed Fletcher became the hero of a tale that belongs in the Luck and Pluck series by Horatio Alger. Things would go wrong, but not very wrong, and so many things would go right. He was 6 feet 3 inches, 16 years old, blue-eyed, and handsome.

"I was already a salesman," Fletcher wrote, "having sold apples, potatoes and farm produce successfully around [Ayer] and in Lowell."

For the last seven days, he'd looked out train windows at prairies and deserts where no cars had been driven, where there was no idea, yet, of cars. The state of Oklahoma had just barely been opened to non-Indian settlement. The streets of San Diego were still dirt. The population of the town he entered had recently collapsed to 16,000. The Hotel del Coronado had been open for just one year, Wyatt Earp lived on Third Avenue, and Ed's shoes scuffed wooden sidewalks that smelled like dung.

In the San Diego Trust & Savings Bank, Ed Fletcher met a cashier named M.T. Gilmore, who asked, "Where are you from?"

It turned out that Gilmore was a fellow pioneer from New England. He gave Ed a job cleaning the cellar of his house and mowing the lawn. Three days later, on Saturday, Mr. Gilmore (who would soon be called Uncle Myron, whom Ed would honor by naming a son Stephen Gilmore Fletcher) gave Ed a five-dollar gold piece. By Monday, Ed had a job with a plumbing firm called Johnson and Patterson. But no story can be all pluck and luck. There must be disappointment, especially when the hero, in all his photographs, looks invincible.

"I was an awkward, overgrown boy and broke eighteen lamp chimneys on Tuesday. Friday I put a 2-inch brass water faucet high on the shelf, and not too secure. Mr. Johnson came along and just happened to be beneath when a jar of the rack forced the water faucet to fall and hit him squarely on the head. We carried him out unconscious and bleeding. That Saturday night I was fired and sobbed most of the way home."

On Monday, Ed Fletcher walked into the produce firm of Nason and Smith, where Mr. Nason and Mr. Smith were arguing about the price paid for 200 boxes of apples. They looked at Ed and said they weren't hiring, but Ed thought about all those apples sitting there and went back in. He said he could sell them fast, before they decayed, if they would loan him a horse and wagon.

"I was asked by Mr. Nason to return the next morning by seven o'clock, and sure enough he furnished me with a wagon and a big mare, and 30 boxes of apples."

He sold 54 boxes the first day, made a profit, and got the job he would keep for eight years, the job that would send him on foot, horseback, wagon, and bicycle across an enormous, naked county that went east to Yuma and north to Perris. Under blue-and-white mackerel skies, during lilac season, in the months when rabbits were having their young, and on summer days when the Santa Ana winds chapped everything, he bought grain, eggs, butter, honey, beeswax, and chicken from the general stores of remote towns like Fallbrook and Hemet and sold them flour, sugar, and canned goods. Accounts were settled once a year, and in 1890, he earned $2.50 a day, twice the daily wage of a laborer. Dinner cost him 25 cents, and a wool suit $13.50.

Ed Sr. at 18

By the time Ed was 18, he was making a monthly trip to the northern edge of the county. He took the morning train to Riverside, did two hours of business there, then rode the train to San Jacinto, arriving at 4:00 p.m. General stores were open in the evenings, so he could still do business at dusk. The next morning he rode his bicycle to Hemet, Perris, and Temecula, arriving in Fallbrook by nightfall with orders in his pocket. From Fallbrook he rode to Bonsall, Vista,

San Marcos, and Escondido.

"There were no bridges across the San Luis Rey River, so unless the river was too high I would first undress and carry my clothes across, then go back and carry my bicycle. The worst problem on my entire trip was to cover the ground from Vista to San Marcos over the worst adobe in California, which in wet weather forced me to carry my bicycle on my back."

He also rode his bicycle to Ramona and Julian, walking beside the bike and pushing it up Mussey Grade. On his first trip he met Joe Foster, the owner and driver of the six-horse stage, which took passengers from the end of the Cuyamaca Railroad to the mountain towns. The trip from San Diego to Julian, which now takes an hour and a half, took 12 hours in 1890, and Joe Foster, who was carrying three passengers on the day he first met Ed Fletcher, gave Ed and his bicycle a free lift to Ramona, Witch Creek, Santa Ysabel, and Julian. In time, Nason and Smith became Smith, Fletcher & Company.

Back in town, Ed went to church with the man he now called Uncle Myron. At 17, Ed had become a member of the First Congregational Church — despite what they said about Unitarians going to hell. By the time he was 22 years old, he was captain of the church's Boys' Brigade. One of his brigadiers, a 20-year-old solicitor for Smith, Fletcher & Company, was Leon Ferner, "a young friend in whom I was very much interested." Leon was an occasional smoker, "and in those days anyone who smoked cigarettes," Fletcher said in his memoir, "was bound for purgatory. I did everything I could to break him of the habit."

On Sunday, September 15, 1895, Leon, Ed, and a Mr. and Mrs. McGegin drove to Ocean Beach. It was a nine-mile, three-hour wagon trip, but the forecast was fair weather. By two o'clock, the three men were swimming out to sea. Ed, who was the tallest, could just barely touch bottom. McGegin and Ed told Leon the undertow was too strong, but Leon seemed not to hear them, and he swam about seven yards farther. A few minutes later, Ed called to him

again, and Leon said he could hardly make headway. He was trying
to swim back to shore, but he wasn't getting any closer.

By then, the undertow had dragged all three men 200 yards
north toward False Bay, which was later dredged and re-shaped to
become the safe, interlocking harbors of Mission Bay. McGegin and
Ed tried to pull Leon closer to the shore in breakers that were ten
feet high. Leon clung to the shoulder of Ed's bathing suit while Ed
tried to swim, but the waves rolled them over and over. "Don't leave
me," Leon said, but an enormous wave knocked them underwater
and pulled them apart. Leon didn't surface again.

Ed had swallowed a lot of water, so when he couldn't find Leon,
he swam out beyond the breakers, floated on his back, coughed up
water, and rested until he could swim to a sandbar, where three men
helped him and McGegin walk out of the water.

"A full account of it was published in the paper the next day,
how I had tried to save my friend's life," Fletcher wrote, and the *San
Diego Union* of September 16 does say that Ed Fletcher nearly died
in the undertow. But despite this proof of his efforts, Ed explained,
he was summoned to the First Congregational Church, where all
the deacons had assembled. "To my amazement they had me sign
my resignation as Captain of the Boys' Brigade on the grounds
that I had set a bad example by going swimming on Sunday." He
was resentful and humiliated at his dismissal for a long time. Leon
Ferner's body was found in False Bay on November 5, 1895, by a
duck hunter.

In the late fall of 1895, evening waists and dresses were sold by
Mr. Bowen on Fifth Street, and C.W. Stults, a few doors down, sold
Dr. Deimel's linen-mesh underwear: "porous and pliable." The San
Diego Cracker Bakery was open on Fourth Street. The Fortnightly
Club of Coronado met on Friday, November 1, at the home of Miss
Agnes Babcock to hear an interesting paper on Churchill, first Duke
of Marlborough. A good set of teeth cost $7, the same price as an
iron bedstead. Fifteen acres of "fine lemon land" on Point Loma

was offered at $1000. The *San Diego Union* observed that an English retriever had captured the hearts of those who walked the grounds of the Hotel del Coronado, and the "highest of all in leavening power" was Royal Baking Powder — "Absolutely Pure."

After work, Ed wrote letters to Mary. He collected wild ferns and pressed them in a book for her, spelling her name with fronds on the last page. They were married on April 8, 1896, in Ayer, Massachusetts, when Mary was 20 and Ed was 23. A friend gave them a copper cowbell engraved with the date, and it was tied to their hack when they drove to the train station. It made, Ed remembered, a tremendous noise.

Mary and Ed Sr., wedding day

This time, Ed Fletcher arrived in San Diego with a wife and $526. He and Mary stayed with the Gilmores, who lived on the corner of Fourth and Beech. He borrowed $1500 after a friend guaranteed the loan, and for $15 a month he rented a store near the southwest corner of Fifth and J Street. Mary kept the books, and Ed sold fruit boxes and flour on commission. In 1898, when their first child was a year old, a photographer came to record the first incarnation of the

Ed Fletcher Company. The sign on the roof says, "Purity, Strength, Color / Port Costa Mills Flour Has No Equal." On the dusty street, women in long dresses and men in vests and bowler hats stand like monuments, and not even the horses move their heads.

As the Ed Fletcher Company grew, Ed gathered his family to San Diego. His sister Bess and her husband Jarvis Doyle, who had gone north to San Francisco, came back and joined the business. Another sister took over the bookkeeping so that Ed's wife could tend the baby. Ed brought Belle, the sister who was still living at the odious Kimball farm, west to San Diego, and Mary Fletcher hauled her father-in-law Charles Fletcher up to Boston and put him on a train to California. Ed built a house for his sister Belle and his father in Lemon Grove. The family history doesn't say whether Charles Fletcher continued to drink, but it does say that Ed Fletcher insisted that no liquor be served at his wedding reception, an insistence that pleased his wife.

Ed Sr.'s produce company, near Fifth and J

Soon the sign over the brick arches said, "Fletcher-Doyle Co. Wholesale Produce," and the brothers-in-law were shipping 181 carloads of lemons and oranges to the East. In the photograph of the Fletcher-Doyle Company, it was horses that waited to haul produce, not trucks. The wheels of the wagons stood perfectly still, as they would stand in the yards of sentimental people 50 years hence. Beneath them, the road was soft dirt and pulverized manure that rose up to cover black clothes.

Fletcher began to compete with John D. Spreckels in the import business, acting as the agent of a San Francisco company that sent shiploads of barley and wheat to Europe and imported Belgian and French cement. "I furnished any amount of cement," Fletcher said, "to San Bernardino, Riverside, Fresno and Bakersfield, Santa Ana, Orange and Anaheim." Fletcher also sold pig iron, coke, fruit-wrapping paper, and the Julian apple crop.

As the 19th Century became the 20th, Fletcher made a decision. "I had made considerable money with the growing business," he wrote, "but never was satisfied. My love of the backcountry, its possibilities of development, both land and water, had a strong appeal to me. I determined to make land and water my life work."

Which, to great success, he did. In 1902, he rode a horse up Hot Springs Mountain (a few miles east of Warner Hot Springs) so he could see the Imperial Valley. He asked the owner of the homestead, which was surrounded by Los Coyotes Indian Reservation, why the land was called Eagle's Nest. The owner said it was because of an Indian legend in which a month-old baby was lying on a blanket beside an adobe hut. An eagle flew down, grabbed the baby like a rabbit in its talons, and flew toward the tree where, a few weeks later, some members of the tribe found a nest that contained the baby's bones and blanket.

It was beautiful land, Fletcher thought, and his wife agreed that it was like Massachusetts, a place where they could plant eastern lilac, chestnuts, and a hard maple tree. Fletcher bought Eagle's Nest from the homesteader for $50 down and $25 a month "until paid for."

In August, 1903, Fletcher, now 30 years old, rode his bicycle to Pala. He'd gotten his start in the land business, but he was still selling produce, and Frank Salmons, the Pala grocer, was one of his customers. Frank asked Fletcher to stay the night and hunt quail with him the next day, so they left the Pala mission the next morning in a buggy.

While Frank and Ed rode to the Pauma Ranch, the wheels of the buggy cracked the arms of tumbleweeds, crushed dry coyote dung, sent whiptail lizards dry-swimming into the brush. When they climbed down from the buggy, they flushed quail out of the bushes, hundreds and hundreds of quail. "Never will I forget," Fletcher wrote, "the excitement of the hunt."

Ed Fletcher Sr. on summit of Grossmont in 1904

In the winter of 1904, he was rich enough to buy the 200-acre Villa Caro Ranch, a house and property that included the hill they would name Grossmont for his partner William B. Gross. Fletcher suggested to Gross that they subdivide because the land was free of frost and city taxes — perfect land for lemons, oranges, and avocados. The *San Diego Union* congratulated Fletcher on his possession of the "noted" Villa

Caro Ranch, and on a clear day, Ed Fletcher posed for a photograph on the summit of Grossmont while wearing his usual three-piece suit and hat. He put his hands in his pockets and surveyed what would be, in many ways, his kingdom. He and Mary and the children (three of them, all very young) had been living in Lemon Grove, where small garter snakes and pollywogs came out of the kitchen faucet. They had retired to the country so Ed could recover from a nervous breakdown and ulcer trouble. Now they could move to the big house at Villa Caro. They could walk among mulberry trees and peacocks while eating their own tangerines.

He and Mike Dooley, the foreman, started to lay out the roads on Grossmont. While they were tying rags on bushes, something happened that would be told again and again in the legend of Ed Fletcher. Fletcher told the story this way in his memoir:

> One afternoon, Dooley was showing me over the path; I was ahead and without seeing, stepped over a rattlesnake; Dooley gave a yell; I looked around; was mad to have done such a thing and tried to kill it with a stone but missed and that made me really mad. As the snake ran into a crack in a rock, I grabbed it by the tail and threw it on the ground and killed it. How Mike Dooley, with tobacco juice dripping from each corner of his mouth, used to love to tell this story!

The story of the snake turns up again in the words of his son, Ed Jr., who was four years old when his father bought Villa Caro. Ed Jr. wrote to his grandson that he carried pieces of white cloth to tie on bushes according to his father's directions, and one day, the two of them stirred up a big rattlesnake.

"It started to rattle and I can remember my dad grabbing rocks and throwing them at the snake, but he missed. The snake started to get away by going amongst some rocks and Dad was so mad he missed him that he reached down and grabbed his tail and shook him out of the rocks, snapping the snake at the same time, and actually killed that rattlesnake with his bare hands. Don't you ever try it."

Ed Sr. became the president of the Volcan Water Company and began to build Warner's Dam, which formed Lake Henshaw. The new owner of Warner Ranch, William Henshaw, put up the money, and Fletcher worked for 25 percent of the net profits on the water project. "I made more money out of this transaction," Fletcher said, "than any during my lifetime."

With a partner, he acquired large tracts of land around Lake Cuyamaca. He acquired the lake itself. When it was cold enough, he skated out on the ice with his children, telling them, perhaps, about the black ice in Massachusetts.

Harry Taylor, Ed Jr., Charlie, Lawrence, and Ed Sr.
skating at Cuyamaca Lake, 1916

With a small down payment, he bought the 2000 acres that would become Fletcher Hills. He built a road to Eagle's Nest, and his family, which by 1910 included Catherine, Ed Jr., Charles, Lawrence, Willis, and Stephen, began to camp there. In 1913 the first road to the summit of Grossmont was finished, and a La Mesa newspaper dubbed the project "Freaky Fletcher's Fancy Flight."

Ed Fletcher's first home at Eagle's Nest

By 1915, all but the last child had been born. Ed Jr. was almost the age his father had been when he first came to San Diego. In 1915, the year of the exposition in Balboa Park, the family had its photo taken on the lawn of their Ash Street house, where Stephen, Ferdinand, Mary Louise, and Eugene had been born, where Mary made bread on Saturday mornings, where servants and children moved through the sunlight and darkness of 27 rooms. On hot summer nights the boys took to the sleeping porch, tired from working (which Ed Jr. did from the age of five), tennis, basketball, swimming, and surfing on wooden boards. At the Ash Street house, there was a tennis court and a pen of guinea pigs that smelled like sweet pine and urine. All of this is gone now, except for the dust it became under the El Cortez Hotel.

You can see, in the photograph, why the word "dynasty" became attached to them. This was, after all, the time of the Romanovs, who looked, like this family, too beautiful for death. The camera records that Catherine, who is 18 in the eternal present of the photograph, has a dimple, that baby Eugene has his mother's eyebrows, that Mary, who was said to use a little buggy whip when order was required, has achieved nine heads of wet combed hair and clean white collars.

Ed, who sits beside her, is now 42 and tanned. In one year, he'll head the construction of the Lake Hodges Dam. In 1926, he and his oldest son will drive from San Diego to Savannah and break the transcontinental auto record by 11 hours and 56 minutes. In 1928, a year before Black Tuesday, he'll be worth $3 million. After the crash, the land and improvements in Fletcher Hills will be assessed at $58,760, but the bonds, coupons, and taxes against the property will total nearly $1 million. Ed will raise $56,000 in 48 hours to pay the assessment and avoid bankruptcy. In 1935, he'll be a state senator. In 1946, there will be three houses in Fletcher Hills. A committee will name Mary the Outstanding California Mother of 1949, and a year later, the *San Diego Journal* will call the Fletchers the "fabulous first family of the city" and boast "clan records unmarked by divorces or deaths."

In August of 1969, when Ed Fletcher, Sr. has been dead 14 years, his ten children will sell the 10,500 acres still owned by the Ed Fletcher Company and appraised at $15 million. They will all be millionaires, but they will also be other things: a cattle rancher, a lawyer, the president of HomeFed, the owner of an insurance company, an Air Force colonel who led the bombing of Rome in 1944 while wounded. Five of the boys will be ex-champion swimmers, former record holders in the breast stroke and the underwater plunge.

Here on the lawn, Ed Sr.'s lips are pale and dry against tanned cheeks. His hands engulf the hands of Mary Louise, who is three. She stands between his knees in a sailor dress and buttoned boots. She leans into him as into an armchair. All the children and their mother look to the right of the photographer's lens, but the Colonel looks directly, steadily into it.

TROUBLE

From the summit of Grossmont, where a carved memorial stone to Ed and Mary Fletcher says, "Our dreams came true," you can hear the hush of wheels on asphalt. It's the sound you hear when you put a conch to your ear. The freeways curl and uncurl toward the white-gold surface of the sea. The tiny roofs of cars are the only things moving between malls, churches, schools, and houses, houses, houses.

The monument, which is on private property, is protected by a very old looped wire fence and shaded by the leaves of a navel orange tree. Magnolias, ice plant, grape vines, purple lantana, geraniums, and lizards brush against the stone, which is taller than a two-story house. A staircase was chiseled into the boulder, which makes the steps look like they were gouged out of clay with bare hands. At the top of the steps, rust darkens granite where it was pierced by poles. The marble plaque lies below, facing the garden. From the summit of the boulder, you can read "Happy Memories" upside down.

How ancient the sea looks from the top of that stone. It's a pale, hazy gold, and it looks vacant, more vacant than the hills and flatlands of San Diego when the photographer put his eye to the glass and made a negative of Colonel Ed Fletcher in his three-piece suit. The land where he stood is now thoroughly "developed," and although, in the early years, he used the term to mean land for peaches, grapes, sugar beets, walnuts, and gladiolas as well as houses, development means concrete now, and beyond the miles of hard, usable roads the sea looks old and foreign, like it still might produce Jesus or Cortez.

The Mt. Helix cross looks very smooth on the opposite hill, which, like Grossmont, once belonged to Ed Fletcher Sr. He donated the summit of Mt. Helix for the nature theater, which was the project of a woman named Mary Yawkey White. In a silent black-and-white film of the 1924 groundbreaking ceremony, Ed Fletcher Sr. is the master of ceremonies. He pantomimes and mouths an introduction of Mrs. White to a crowd of women in fur-trimmed coats. A bottle of champagne breaks and foams. No trees shade the summit, and the valleys scanned by the camera are bare.

During the next year, Ed Fletcher Jr. and his crew drilled into rock, formed the concrete steps and benches of the amphitheater, and poured white Medusa cement into the wooden form of a 35-foot cross. On Easter morning, 1925, 8000 people came to see the theater that had been built at the cost of $100,000 and dedicated to the "inspiration and use of the people."

The nature theater is shady now, but the views are of suburbia, not nature. The cross that Ed Jr.'s crew poured more than 70 years ago is protected by a thick hedge and a padlocked gate. The stone marker explains that the cross was built with private funds as a memorial to Mary Carpenter Yawkey, that the ground beneath it is owned by the San Diego Historical Society, and that no public funds maintain the cross. Furthermore, "the display of this cross by the San Diego Historical Society is for memorial and historical purposes, and is in no way intended to be an endorsement of preference of any religious belief." The cross with its disclaimer looks threatened and defensive. The paint is fresh, but the monument is sacred to a smaller group now, one that wants to remember how things used to be.

Ed Sr. and Mary's memorial stone

The cross isn't a monument to Ed Fletcher Sr., but it's a good metaphor for what happened to his name. His son built the cross and became its keeper, as he was the keeper of the Colonel's memory and the family records. For many years, he was paid $200 to keep the nature theater free of vandalism (the memorial plaque was repeatedly pried off and stolen). Every spring, he took his sons up Mt. Helix to clean for the Easter service. In retirement, he spent years doing the Fletcher genealogy, traveling to the places in Massachusetts that his father described in his memoir. When he was 88, he told a *San Diego Union* reporter, "They never made [another] one like him. That's why I never dropped the Junior in my name."

It's also why he named his firstborn Ed III, never dreaming there would come a time when the greatest threat to the family honor would come from him. When Ed Jr. died on Christmas day, 1996, his death was front-page news in the *Union-Tribune*. To the fury of some family members and friends, the story about his life noted that his son, Edward Fletcher III, was serving a life sentence for murder. *Why couldn't the newspaper be silent about that one fact?*

they wondered. Why couldn't Ed Jr. be remembered for his father and not his son?

The pluck-and-luck storyline had been turned into something else. "Look how he prospered!" became "What happened?" The inspirational story became a cautionary tale.

Ed Jr. with wife Mildred and their sons,
Edward III, Michael, and Larry

In 1990, three years before the murders of Walter and Carrlene Harper, an interviewer for the San Diego Historical Society asked Ed Jr. if he had been as hard on his boys as his father had been on him.

"I feel I should have been a little tougher on my children than I was, but I didn't have the heart to be the taskmaster that my dad was," Ed Jr. said. "I tried to teach them to do unto others as you would have them do unto you."

In 1995, two years after the murders, another interviewer for the historical society asked Ferdinand Fletcher, the uncle of Ed III, "in a great family like yours with so many people who are always doing everything nice, what happened to Ed III, who got off on the wrong track and became an alcoholic and loused up the whole business? Were there others who went that way and never got into real trouble, or was he the only one?"

"I am sure there were others," Ferdinand Fletcher said, "but nothing like that." Ferdinand said that he and his siblings lived responsibly because they didn't want to disappoint their parents, who had been so good to them. "None of us," he said, "wanted to let them down."

Perhaps there was a time when Ed III felt the same, but if the public record of the three generations were to be bound in separate books, Ed Sr.'s would be as large and quaint as an old dictionary, Ed Jr.'s would be a thick, annotated scrapbook, and Ed III's would be a long shelf of legal documents. The public facts about his childhood fit in a single paragraph. He grew up in Mission Beach and Grossmont, and he worked weekends on his father's thousand-acre ranch in El Cajon. In the usual manner of brothers, he made his little brother, who hated riding, ride old Clabberlip, the Mexican saddle pony. He went to a private school called the Boyden School, which advertised itself as a boys' high school that offered Annapolis and West Point preparatory courses. He liked to sneak out of school, which was near the old California Theater on Fourth Avenue, and watch movies. In the tradition of the Fletcher men, he learned to hunt. He learned to fish. His holidays were spent at paradises won: Cuyamaca, Eagle's Nest, Del Mar. He grew up the grandson of a man who knew Theodore Roosevelt, Warren Harding, and Herbert Hoover, a man who had been a guest in the presidential palace of Mexico, who entertained senators, college presidents, admirals, generals, and millionaires, who had killed a rattlesnake with his bare hands and had swum into the Del Mar surf to haul in a 37-pound shark that had tried to steal his fishing rod. As a boy, Ed III went on one of his grandfather's many fishing trips off the coast of Mexico. In one photograph, he's the smallest boy in the group, his face shaded by a baseball cap. The rest of him is obscured by a group that includes an attorney general and a governor.

In 1951, the second year of the Korean War, Ed III was photographed beside an AT-6 at Lackland Air Force Base in San Antonio, Texas. There beside the propeller, he smiles and squints. He's the third generation in uniform, part of a chapter in the Colonel's book called "The War Record of Our Boys." Another photograph of him in uniform, this one an eight-by-ten of his head and shoulders, would be tinted, framed, and kept on a table by his father's chair even after he went to prison.

In 1952, Ed III married Marjorie Jean Berlin, the only child of a well-to-do family who lived on old Fletcher territory: Mt. Helix. They were married on her birthday in the spring. Marjorie had graduated the year before from San Diego State, where she was a sorority girl who wrote skits and poems, the secretary of her senior class cabinet, and a member of the debating team. In time, her husband would hit her.

Ed III and Marjorie had three sons. They raised them in Borrego Springs, where they lived at the Borrego Air Ranch, a flat stretch of land developed by his father Ed Jr. in 1946. It's a small subdivision built around the principle of flight: houses on the edge of an airstrip, one hangar to a house. Ed III, like his father and grandfather, sold real estate. He built his own house. He flew his own plane, shot ducks in Idaho and doves in Borrego, and was considered by members of his family to be a safe, careful, extremely accurate hunter. They said he never drank when he was hunting. Never.

Audrey Hibdon, Marjorie's housekeeper and friend for more than 15 years, thinks the drinking increased after Ed and Marjorie's three sons graduated from high school. A neighbor who moved to the air ranch in the 1980s declared under penalty of perjury that he, his wife, and the Fletchers went to dinner one night. Afterward, while in the neighbor's home, "Edward Fletcher began to beat Marjorie Fletcher." The neighbor intervened, Ed crashed into a table, and the table broke. The next day, the neighbor said, Ed Fletcher apologized to him.

Ed III in Air Force, 1951

By the time former county supervisor Paul Fordem moved to the Borrego Air Ranch in the early 1990s, the Fletcher name was associated in Borrego Springs with "the man and woman that drank to excess." Ed's own cousin told Fordem, who knew most of the Fletcher family through his 22 years of employment at the Fletcher-owned Home Federal Savings and Loan, "Stay away from Ed. He's a no-good drunk."

But Fordem never had any trouble with Ed, who dropped by two or three times a week to offer advice when Fordem was building his house. The Fordems and the Fletchers had lunch two or three times at each other's houses, and Fordem saw none of the abuse that people told him about. They all drank iced tea because the Fordems knew the Fletchers had trouble with alcohol, and Paul Fordem sympathized with that. "It is a disease, in my belief," he said. Ed insisted that the Fordems take fill dirt from his property for the house pad. Ed refused to take any money for the dirt, and when Marjorie decided to have a dinner party on the eve of the annual dove hunt, she called the Fordems and invited them to come.

On the afternoon of August 31, 1993, Eric Fletcher, whom housekeeper and friend Audrey Hibdon called "the good son," was on his way to Borrego Springs to attend that dinner and the dove hunt. Eric was 35. His brother Kent was also on his way to the house in Borrego Springs, but he was not invited. According to Hibdon, Kent had been kicked out of the house at 18 and told by his father to "go give somebody else some grief." In August of 1991, Kent had broken into his parents' house, pointed a gun at his mother, and robbed them. That fall, Kent pleaded guilty to seven counts of robbery, assault, and false imprisonment and was released on probation.

PHOTO BY SANDY HUFFAKER JR.

The name Borrego Air Ranch is spelled out in iron letters over the entrance. The sign is tooth-white and decorated with iron curlicues. The private drive it announces, Fletcher Road, is nothing fancy. The palm trees along one side of the asphalt are stubby and have an untended look. The mobile homes and ranch houses, about 20 in all, look disorderly from a distance because the airplane hangars are large and plain and because in the desert, very little that is man-made looks permanent or natural. The air ranch is a place where the survival of anything imported is up to you and where summer heat will kill anything you're not there to save. So the view along the dirt and asphalt roads is of decorative cow skulls, greasewood, ocotillo, pale windsocks, swimming pools behind glass walls, and wide, wide airplane hangars. Sometimes the houses have numbers, sometimes not. You'd have to know where you were going to find somebody here.

Fifteen years before, when the Fletcher boys were still in school, Audrey Hibdon had come to the Fletchers' house at the air ranch every Wednesday. Hibdon and Marjorie had often gone shopping together and driven to Mt. Helix to take Marjorie's mother out to lunch. But after the youngest son left home, Ed and Marjorie drank more. Hibdon cleaned less—once every two weeks instead of every week. She had a key to the house because if the Fletchers went out of town, she took care of Ed's Brittany spaniels, his hunting dogs.

"In the last 18 years," Audrey Hibdon said, "there've been times when I felt . . . I've come home and told my husband, 'You know, it's possible I'd be an alcoholic too if I was in love with a man like that, and lived with a man like that.'" She saw that Marjorie had bruises and that there were more bruises as time went on. She also saw that Marjorie loved Ed and couldn't imagine her life without him. When Hibdon had what she called a few loud squabbles with Ed, "real loud arguments," and quit, Marjorie begged Hibdon to come back. Ed promised to stay out of her way, and Hibdon resumed work.

She had cleaned the Fletcher house on the previous Thursday, so on Tuesday morning, August 31, she was just coming to help Marjorie tidy up and make dinner for the guests. When she arrived at 8:00 a.m., she realized she'd forgotten her key. She had to ring the doorbell, and Ed answered the door. According to her courtroom testimony, he asked her where the heck her key was.

"He was so drunk he could hardly stand," Hibdon told me, "and he had been into the village that morning at seven o'clock to pick up donuts for the bird breakfast the next morning, and they told me down there that he was so drunk they handed him the box and asked him to come back tomorrow and pay because they were trying to get him out of the business."

While cleaning, she saw bottles of vodka, Beefeater's gin, and

Cutty Sark. She put them under the wet bar. She believed that the Fletchers had both been up all night drinking, but she cleaned the kitchen and vacuumed. She set the dining room table to the sound of voices from Ed's television in the back bedroom. Marjorie came into the kitchen and asked Hibdon to light a cigarette for her. It was not like other days, when Marjorie made chicken-fried steak because it was Hibdon's favorite, or read aloud from the journals she'd kept since she first met Ed.

"She used to read to me," Hibdon said, "while I was, oh, scrubbing and polishing the kitchen, or whatever I was doing at the time, and she would read these journals to me, and they were just fantastic. You almost felt like you were there." But on this morning, Hibdon put her arms around Marjorie's waist and walked her back to bed. She decided it would be pointless to prepare food for a dinner party.

In the bedroom, in its usual place, was an antique shotgun that had belonged to Marjorie's mother. Baby pictures of the three boys. In the walk-in closet that belonged to Ed, there was another shotgun. In the room called the office or the den, a room near the front door, there was another walk-in closet used to store guns. It was usually locked tight, but she had seen inside the closet once or twice, seen the rifles, shotguns, and boxes of ammunition. The living room was decorated with Marjorie's framed family photographs and Ed's stuffed animal heads — wild boar, deer, mountain sheep.

On her way out the door, Hibdon spoke to Ed, who was standing in the kitchen. "I don't think you're going to be able to serve dinner," she said, "and so I won't be back." She suggested they go someplace else for dinner, but she doesn't remember his response.

Besides Eric, his wife, and the Fordems, there were two other dinner guests, Walter and Carrlene Harper. At nine o'clock the same morning, the Harpers met two friends at the Mission Bay Golf Course for their regular biweekly game.

Walter had graduated from La Jolla High School in 1946, had run his own sign company downtown, and then worked as an electrician until he retired. A former lifeguard who still looked seaworthy and benevolent, he rode his bike three times a week to the Mission Beach Plunge to do his regular workout. He'd been married for 39 years and 8 months to Carrlene, a retired medical school administrator with whom he had raised two children, Grant and Lisa. "They were more in love the day they died," Lisa told *San Diego* magazine, "than the day they married."

While they golfed, Walter and Carrlene talked about their plans for the afternoon. Marjorie Fletcher had called the week before and invited them to be houseguests, as they had been the year before, and the year before that. Marjorie sounded, Carrlene thought, like she'd been drinking. The Harpers had been planning to spend the night at La Casa del Zorro, a resort near the air ranch, but Marjorie wouldn't hear of it. "No, there's no reason for you to do that," she said. "We want you to stay here. We absolutely insist upon it."

White balls on the fairway. Carts moving forward, stopping, and moving again. Carrlene explained that she had finally accepted the invitation because they were the only friends the Fletchers had left. The others stayed away because the Fletchers drank too much. The dove hunt was a tradition, they went every year, and they really were old friends (the Harper children had camped at Eagle's Nest with the Fletcher children). Besides, the Harpers and the Fletchers had a pact: they would see each other only if the Fletchers were sober. If things got difficult, they could always go stay at La Casa del Zorro.

Instead of staying for lunch after the 18th hole, the Harpers went straight home because "if they were late getting to the Fletchers," a friend testified, "Ed would be angry."

Twenty months earlier, in late December of 1991, a clinical psychologist named Judy and her boyfriend Briar were invited to spend New Year's Eve at the Fletcher house. Judy had met Marjorie and Ed before, and she didn't like them. She thought they drank too much and that Ed seemed antagonistic and unstable. She told

Briar she didn't want to go, but Briar felt sorry for them because they didn't have any friends. Briar promised to cancel the plans, but when he called Ed to say they couldn't come, Ed insisted. Briar and Judy agreed to spend the night.

When they arrived between five and six o'clock, the house was dark. There appeared to be no dinner. Only Ed was there to entertain them because Marjorie was "passed out in the bedroom." Judy was extremely uncomfortable. Briar suggested that it probably wasn't a good time for a visit, and maybe they should get together another time.

"No, you're my houseguests," Ed said. "You're going to stay."

Judy would testify that this was not a suggestion but a command. Ed invited Briar to put on his swimsuit and sit in the Jacuzzi, which he did. A little while later, when Ed went to the bedroom to wake up Marjorie, "to try to rouse Marge to join us," Briar and Judy saw their chance to leave. They got into their truck, locked the doors, and drove away. When Ed came back to the living room, no one was there.

Eric Fletcher and his wife Beatrice had attended the dove hunt together three or four times. Eric hunted, and Beatrice read magazines, talked to the other women, played with the spaniels. They left their two children, who were eight and six at the time, at home not because the Fletchers were alcoholics but because of the guns. Prior to August of 1993, the Fletchers didn't drink when Eric, Beatrice, and the grandchildren came to visit.

When Eric and Beatrice reached the house, it was late afternoon, and the Harpers had already arrived. Ed and Walter were standing in front of the carport, and by the way Ed said hello, Beatrice could tell he'd been drinking. "He seemed overly — overly kind and sweet and kind of sloppy," she told the prosecutor, "kind of, 'oh, I love you so much.'"

Beatrice went to the room she would have shared with Eric that night if everyone had just gone to the meeting, had dinner, said good night, and fallen asleep. She was unpacking when Carrlene Harper, happy to have company and to see Beatrice again, came in to say hello. She told Beatrice that Marjorie was passed out in her bedroom, that the food for dinner was sitting in the fridge unprepared, and that Ed was three sheets to the wind.

All this way, and no dinner. Eric and his wife had driven from El Cajon. The Harpers had driven from Pacific Beach. Not just that, but the humiliation to Eric. Beatrice said she knew it was very upsetting to him.

Sometime between 4:30 and 5:30 p.m., the family situation, already tense, got worse. Eric's brother Kent, the one who had robbed his parents in this very house two years earlier, came to the side door and pounded on it, asking for money.

On August 18, Kent had entered Grossmont Hospital "for mental problems possibly related to methamphetamine use," according to the county probation report. While there, Kent told the social worker he intended to kill his uncle, Lawrence Fletcher. He threatened a staff member with a claw hammer and was taken by hospital security to the county mental health facility. The next day, he climbed a patio wall and escaped. Because a doctor there considered him dangerous, an arrest warrant was requested on August 20. Three days later, Kent's probation officer found him at home and ordered him to appear at the probation office that evening for a drug test. The request for a warrant was withdrawn because Kent kept that appointment.

Lawrence Fletcher was Ed III's youngest brother — Kent's uncle. He testified that he had assisted Kent in 1992 by giving him money and a place to live — a room in his vacant El Cajon warehouse. "It had a nice little room, a bathroom, a shower and all of the facilities," he said. "So I moved a refrigerator in, hot plate, microwave oven, the necessities of life; gave him a key and told him he could reside there until he got himself back on his feet. Lawrence also urged Kent to enter drug rehabilitation. When Kent returned from the drug treatment program, another uncle gave him some work, but he needed a car, so Lawrence found a broken-down $400 car and helped Kent fix it up on evenings and Saturdays.

Kent paid for the car whenever he could, but then he started, as Lawrence put it, to go downhill again. On two previous occasions, Kent had threatened Lawrence's life. One afternoon near the end of August 1993, Kent came into the warehouse. He looked like he hadn't been working. There was a "glaze" in his eye. Kent and his uncle argued, and then Kent started swinging. "It was all I could do to hold him off," Lawrence testified, "even though he was in this — what I considered a drugged state."

Lawrence called to an employee, who pulled Kent away. Kent left the warehouse, but he began to call his uncle in the middle of the night. Kent threatened to kill him, so Lawrence made an application for a concealed weapons permit.

At midnight on August 24, Kent rang the doorbell at the Fletcher Hills house of his grandfather, Ed Jr. Ed Jr.'s housekeeper testified that Kent asked to come in the house and sleep, but she told him that was against his grandfather's orders. Kent began to shout obscenities at her and then requested a blanket. She awakened Ed Jr., who was then 93 years old, and the two of them took a blanket to the front of the house and shoved it through the partially opened door.

"And when we did that," the housekeeper testified, "Kent stuck his foot in the door so we couldn't close it and shook his fist at me and his grandfather and said, 'You're doomed, old man, and so is your son Larry.'"

Lawrence Fletcher requested a restraining order against Kent on August 27 and called his brother Ed III to tell him what had happened. Since staying away from his parents was a condition of Kent's probation, the restraining order simply expanded the number of family members Kent was prohibited to see.

Three days later, the day before the Harpers and the Fletchers met for the dove hunt in Borrego Springs, Kent Fletcher failed to show up for his next appointment at the probation office, where his August 23 drug test had come back positive for amphetamine and cannabinoid use. On the afternoon of August 31, Kent drove out to the air ranch and knocked on his father's door.

Neither Eric nor Ed opened it. Through the closed door, Kent asked for money to get back to San Diego, and Ed refused. Kent was angry, Eric testified, but he made no threats. Eric told his wife, who had heard loud voices from the opposite end of the house, that Kent had driven away, but his visit rattled her.

"It sounds kind of silly," she testified. "I had gotten magazines, and I was going to sit down and lay down on the bed and read. And all of a sudden I just had — I don't know, I just got nervous that I had the lights on in the house and all the blinds and the windows were wide open. I had kind of envisioned Kent sneaking back after he had been shooed away and was concerned that, since there were no houses down that way, if he were going to go hide his car anywhere, that would be back in that area. So, I just had concerns and shut the drapes." Her concerns, she explained, were based on threats of violence. In the past, Kent had threatened her and her family with bodily harm, and he had threatened to kill Eric.

Either before or after Kent's visit (Eric testified that he couldn't remember which it was), Eric and his father had an argument. This time, the subject was the meeting of the dove club. Ed was too drunk to go, Eric said. Eric told his father that he should stay home, that he and Beatrice would go to the meeting with the Harpers. Eric assumed that his father agreed, but when everyone else got ready to go, Ed got ready too. If Ed was going, Eric said, then he was staying home. It was too embarrassing to be with his father in public.

Ed III's house at Borrego Air Ranch

Ed Fletcher left for the meeting with the Harpers, and Eric looked around the house. He found a full bottle of gin and a nearly empty half-gallon of vodka beneath the kitchen sink. He poured them out and threw the empty bottles in the trashcan by the door, where a police detective would notice them the next day.

"Did you expect to have a confrontation of some type with your father," the prosecutor asked, "when he found out you had poured out the alcohol?"

"I really didn't care if I had a little confrontation with my father about pouring out the alcohol or not," Eric said.

While Beatrice and Eric were talking about packing up and going home, the phone rang. It was Dan Bridge, his father's old friend and a childhood friend of Walter Harper. Dan Bridge was hosting the meeting of the dove-hunting club. Bridge said that Ed III was there at the meeting, and, yes, he'd been drinking, but he was behaving himself and Eric really should come, since Eric was, after all, the president. Eric and Beatrice locked the door behind them when they left for the meeting, which had already started when they arrived.

It wasn't a very long meeting, less than an hour, but every action, every word, would reverberate. It was the last time anyone but Ed Fletcher III saw the Harpers alive. Everything was already wrong — for Eric, Beatrice, Walter and Carrlene, even for Ed and Marjorie Fletcher — but jokes, admonitions, and plans were still possible. People, including Ed III, made light remarks ("Your son's better-looking than you are," he told his cousin) that would be repeated under oath in the Vista County Courthouse, Department B. Sixteen members of the Fletcher family belonged to this club. The six or so who came to the meeting — cousins and uncles — sat in a mobile home they would later be asked to describe for police officers and lawyers because it was the scene that would, to a great extent, determine the guilt and punishment of Ed III.

The predicament of his friends and relatives was at times painfully clear. When asked to affirm that Ed was "jovial" at the meeting, Ed III's uncle Ferdinand said, "He was quite jovial, and he put his arm around me and sort of hugged me a little bit and — I've known him for all of his life."

The testimony about that hour came down to this: was Ed III, at the meeting of the dove club, a rational man? Did he stumble, slur, fall down, or weave? Did he understand what was said to him and respond logically? Did he get angry when people tried to curb his drinking? If he could give a lucid report about the club's dove-feeding operation while his blood alcohol level was approaching .33, could he also premeditate to kill someone? Or was he, despite this lucid report, a man on medication for bipolar disorder, also known as manic-depression, who had been drinking so much for so long that he was permanently brain-damaged, was literally "de-mented," out of his mind? If he recognized every single person at the meeting in Dan Bridge's mobile home, did he hallucinate an hour later in his own house and see not Walter and Carrlene when he pulled the trigger, but his own dangerous son, whom he had armed himself against, and/or the good son, who had poured out his liquor?

Eric testified that his father was not doing anything crazy. He was acting, in Eric's opinion, intoxicated, but he was sitting down and standing up, milling around and chatting like everyone else.

Eric and his father had a conversation at the makeshift bar, which was set up near the kitchen. Eric called it "the first confrontation." Ed III was filling up an eight-ounce plastic glass with Popov vodka, which he had joked to someone else was evidence of a "chintzy operation."

"And I told him that I didn't think he needed any more," Eric testified. "And he said, you know, 'Leave me alone' or 'I'll do what I want' or whatever. And I told him he was embarrassing me and making an ass out of himself and he — you know," Eric gestured with an elbow, "get out of my way."

Beatrice sat with Carrlene in a room beside the living room, where they could see what was going on and still have a separate conversation. Beatrice testified that she tried to ignore Ed's drinking completely because she knew that Eric was embarrassed by it. "Knowing how [Eric] would feel," she said, "I just tried to pretend that it didn't — wasn't there, wasn't going on."

Beatrice told Carrlene about shutting the drapes so that Kent, if he was still at the air ranch, couldn't see her. It was then that Carrlene made the joke that would become terrible.

Carrlene told Beatrice she had a feeling they would read in the newspapers the next day: "FRIENDS FOUND SHOT AT THE FLETCHERS." She wasn't thinking of Ed III as a murderer, Beatrice testified. At that moment, they were both afraid of Kent.

Sometime in the same quarter hour, Carrlene gently chided Ed about his glass of vodka. "That's not water you're drinking, Ed," Beatrice heard Carrlene say. "You don't need to drink that."

Ed grumbled in response, said, "Oh, to hell with you," and walked away.

Ed kept drinking, and Eric failed, for the second time, to stop him. He told his wife, "We're out of here. Let's go." The meeting was over, so the Harpers walked out of the house behind them. Eric and Beatrice went one direction, and the Harpers went the other.

Eric and Beatrice reached the air ranch first and realized they had no key to get in the house. It was about five minutes to seven, and the moon had just started to rise. Paul and Pat Fordem were pulling into the driveway for the dinner party that was supposed to start at seven o'clock. They introduced themselves to Eric and Beatrice, who told them that the dinner was canceled because Mrs. Fletcher wasn't in any condition to host a party, and Ed III, who was on his way home, had been drinking heavily. The sun was still above the horizon, so everyone's face (humiliated, apologetic, sympathetic, or polite) was visible. The Fordems drove up Fletcher Road to the mailboxes, retrieved a neighbor's mail, and went home to make sandwiches. Eric and Beatrice walked to the watering hole to have a look at the birds. Beatrice was relieved to take a walk because she was afraid Kent might be in the house.

The Harpers' car began to approach the house, but at that moment, Beatrice testified, Eric "wasn't real excited about being right with his dad." They waited a few minutes more. Then they started walking home, and when they were 40 yards away, they heard the first shot. Beatrice crouched down on the ground and heard a woman's voice say, "Oh, my God."

"Was this a shriek?" the prosecutor asked. "More a yell or a shriek?"

"It was a shriek," Beatrice said.

Eric testified that he then told Beatrice to run to a hangar on the south side of Stinson Road. She began to run, and when she looked back, she saw Eric crouching and running toward his father's house. Beatrice hid for 20 minutes while Eric watched his father pace with the gun, waited for a safe moment to enter the house, and discovered the bodies on the kitchen floor.

"Oh my God," he said to Beatrice when he found her. "My dad shot the Harpers."

Then they ran again, knocking at two neighboring houses before they decided to try the Fordems. They had just spoken to the Fordems, Beatrice reasoned, so they were sure to be home. The Fordems let them in, and when Paul Fordem heard what had happened, he called 911. "We don't know exactly all the details," Fordem told the dispatcher, "but the man's been drinking heavily and he is armed. And we believe that he has shot at least two people."

The bodies of Walter and Carrlene Harper would be taken from Borrego Springs to Kearny Mesa in sealed pouches. During the examination, coroner Harry Bonnell would find a shotgun entry wound in the middle of Walter's upper chest. He would find gunpowder residue around the wound in a pattern called tattooing or stippling. The skin was charred by the flame that came out of the muzzle of the gun. There were four irregular, jagged exit wounds on the left side of his spine.

"When we removed the shirt," he testified, "two pellets fell out, and we also recovered four pellets from still inside the body, in the back."

These pellets struck Walter Harper's sternum, his ribs, and the left side of his spine. The gun was close enough to Walter's chest to shoot corklike wadding and bits of plastic through the skin. The pellets destroyed part of his trachea and his esophagus. They perforated his aorta, three major blood vessels, and his lung. They fractured his front and back ribs.

The force of the blast itself, Bonnell testified, probably knocked Walter Harper to the floor. "In my opinion, he would be rendered unconscious near immediately. Certainly within 10 to 15 seconds because there would be a total lack of blood supply going to the brain following this injury. And since all the blood being pumped by his heart is going to his chest and not to the rest of his body, in my opinion he would be dead within three to four minutes."

The pellets entered Carrlene Harper's body through the upper portion of her right arm and her right chest, fracturing bone in her fourth, fifth, sixth, and seventh ribs, perforating two of the three lobes of her right lung, and fracturing her spine. They cut her aorta in half and perforated the other lung before making seven irregular, jagged exit wounds that covered an area three inches long and three inches wide.

She was conscious, Bonnell estimated, between 15 and 30 seconds longer than her husband, and while she was conscious, she bled into her chest and lungs. She would not have been able to scream "Oh, my God" after the blast because "if she exhaled, the air would be forced out all of the shotgun pellet holes in her lungs into her chest and out into the air around the chest. And similarly, when she — if she inhaled, she would have what is referred to as a sucking chest wound. In other words, when you inhale, you create negative pressure in your chest, and these holes in the chest would cause the air to rush in there and collapse her lungs down. So, in my opinion, she would not be able to vocalize much of anything above maybe a small whisper with this kind of injury to her lungs."

Deputy Sheriff James McKenna was on call that night when he was informed there had been a shooting at the Fletcher residence. He already knew Ed Fletcher III because he and other deputies had investigated previous complaints at the Borrego Air Ranch, including "random firing from his residence, near and toward adjacent residences; threats of bodily injury to past neighbors; and most recently his arrest for assaulting a Pacific Bell telephone employee with a firearm." While en route, McKenna summoned the San Diego SWAT team and deputies from Borrego Springs, Ranchita, and Julian. He told the Borrego Springs fire department, which was already at the entrance of the air ranch, not to approach the Fletcher house.

Eric and Paul Fordem met McKenna at the entrance of the air ranch, and Eric told McKenna that he had seen "both the Harpers, shot, lying on the floor, dead." McKenna asked how he knew they were dead, not just wounded, and Eric said he knew by their "stares."

By now, it was around eight o'clock. McKenna told Eric to return to Paul Fordem's house and wait there with Beatrice. It was the blue-black end of twilight, and white things glowed in the rising moon. From the intersection of Fletcher Road and Borrego Springs Road, where the white iron sign arcs over the desert, McKenna called the Fletcher house on his cellular phone. McKenna wanted to keep Ed occupied while two officers took their positions outside the house. Both Marjorie and Ed answered the phone, and McKenna asked Ed to come outside, but when McKenna and his sergeant reached the west side of the house, the driveway was empty. McKenna called again and said he'd meet Ed outside.

"Maybe I don't want to do that," Ed said.

McKenna said they needed to talk about what happened.

"Yeah, I guess we should," Ed said.

They agreed to meet outside by a parked van. It was now dark, except for moonlight. McKenna moved on foot to the west wall of the carport because "he could peer directly into the kitchen door." If Ed complied and went to the van, McKenna would have a tactical advantage.

An interior light came on. The door opened, and Ed peeked out. Then he slowly closed the door again.

"Ed!" McKenna shouted.

Ed opened the door again, an exterior floodlight came on, and Ed closed the door.

McKenna shouted, "Ed! It's McKenna!"

It was then that Ed stepped out of the house. Lit by the floodlight, he was wearing beige pants with a thin dark belt. He was barefoot. He was not wearing a shirt. (A criminologist would later testify that Fletcher's white shirt was spotted with human blood of the same type as Walter Harper. She also found a bloodstain on the tip of Fletcher's right shoe.) McKenna wrote in the police report that he could see a lit cigarette in Ed's left hand. As if remembering his destination at last, Ed walked toward the van, and as he moved, McKenna saw that he was unarmed. Still, McKenna walked "gingerly" toward him, and from ten feet away, "called softly to him, 'Ed. It's McKenna.' McKenna continued to walk, saying, "You aren't packing, are you."

With that, McKenna took Ed's right hand. Another deputy approached with handcuffs and took the same arm. When Ed was told to drop the cigarette, he took a last drag and threw it down. He was handcuffed, and after McKenna summoned a caged patrol unit, Ed looked at him and said, "I guess I'm in trouble, huh?"

CONSEQUENCE

Demand me nothing. What you know, you know.
From this time forth I never will speak word.
— Iago in *Othello* V.ii

The criminal trial of Edward Fletcher III began more than a year later, on November 22, 1994. Members of the Fletcher family did not attend except to testify. They stayed away, Ed III's brother Lawrence said, out of respect for the Harpers and because they were ashamed.

A civil suit was pending at the same time. In the early part of the year, Lisa Harper Henderson and Grant Harper, the two adult children of Walter and Carrlene, had filed a $20 million wrongful death case against Ed III and Marjorie, charging that the Harpers were "enticed" to the home and that Marjorie had been negligent in failing to warn them about her husband's violent temper. Ed Fletcher III maintained that he did not remember the shootings. He said that he blacked out after leaving the hunting club and didn't recall anything between the drive home and his arrest.

According to defense witness Mark Kalish, a psychiatrist, Ed Fletcher III suffered from manic-depression, lithium-induced hypothyroidism, and dementia. Dr. Kalish testified that the illness was probably genetic. He felt that Ed was paranoid and delusional and that he wasn't smart enough to fake mental illness during written and oral examinations. The high amount of alcohol in Fletcher's system that night had probably aggravated his tendencies "like pouring alcohol on a raw hand." Kalish said that Ed tended, while examined in his jail cell, to "perseverate" or obsess about a single, insignificant detail even after the conversation had moved on. It was, Kalish said, like a hiccup in the brain. Two other psychiatrists also found Ed Fletcher III to be clinically demented.

Mark J. Mills, a witness for the prosecution who is both a psychiatrist and a Harvard Law School graduate, testified that Fletcher did not suffer from dementia or, in all likelihood, from manic-depression. He found the timing of the blackout "highly coincidental." Dr. Mills explained that delirium generally lasted longer than an hour — the period of time when Ed Fletcher III had no memory — and at the meeting of the hunt club, he was clearly not delirious. Dr. Mills further disagreed with Kalish about Fletcher's capacity to distort the results of his exams. "You don't have to be a rocket scientist," he testified, "to lie."

In all, 36 witnesses testified in a trial that lasted 18 days. On December 16, 1994, the jury that had promised, in the poetic language of the court, to "well and truly try the cause now pending and a true verdict render," found Edward Fletcher III guilty on two counts of first-degree murder with special circumstances. When the defense lawyer requested that the degree of offense be lessened to second-degree murder because there was insufficient evidence to prove that Fletcher "premeditated and deliberated a willful killing of the Harpers," Judge David Moon gave his own conclusions about what happened that night.

Experts in the physical effects of alcohol consumption had persuaded Judge Moon that a person with Ed Fletcher III's tolerance for alcohol could function at a blood-alcohol level so high that most people would be passed out or comatose. He could, therefore, formulate an intent to kill. The intent to kill, the judge reasoned, was manifested by the fact that Ed Fletcher III had ignored the two shotguns in the kitchen that were designed for killing doves and had walked to the bedroom to retrieve a shotgun that could kill geese flying several hundred yards away.

"Premeditation," Judge Moon said, "may take place in a very short period of time. Here the evidence tends to show that, when Mr. Fletcher walked into his own home, he probably saw the empty liquor bottles that were on top of this trash can at the entrance, and that probably set him off. The object of his anger immediately would have been Eric." A rational person, Moon reasoned, would have suspected that Eric, not the Harpers, poured out the liquor. Eric had been alone in the house, and the Harpers had not.

Although Moon conceded that no one would ever know exactly what happened in that house, he (and the jury) could infer from the evidence that Ed probably expressed his anger at Eric, and the Harpers responded by announcing their departure. Carrlene Harper picked up the green telephone book that would be found at her feet by the police. "Now, that, I'm sure, set off Mr. Fletcher again." But now he was angry at the Harpers, not his son. (Ed's brother Lawrence also felt that the departure of the Harpers could have been a final blow — that something in him already distorted by alcohol and lithium snapped when his two remaining friends decided to go elsewhere.)

In the judge's reasoning, Ed left the kitchen, where there were already two unloaded, less dangerous weapons, his own and Eric's. He didn't choose either of these lesser guns, nor did he go to the dining room, where there was another locked gun case full of weapons. He went down a long hall to his bedroom, retrieved an extremely powerful, loaded gun, pointed it at Walter Harper, and fired. He racked the gun, aimed at Carrlene, and fired again.

The difference between first- and second-degree murder, the judge explained, is whether there was "an opportunity for the slayer to weigh and evaluate the consequences of his action."

"Let's take a look at what happened directly after the shooting," he said. "Mr. Fletcher did not do something along these lines: 'My God, what have I done?' or, 'I can't believe that I just shot my best friends. He didn't kneel on the kitchen floor and try to help them."

Instead, he "stalked around the house." His son Eric, standing outside the house, heard his father say, "Where is that son of a bitch?" Although Eric thought at the time that his father was talking about Kent, he later felt that his father was looking for him, and the judge agreed that the evidence made this clear. "He was now angry," the judge said, "still angry at Eric, who just poured out his booze." The judge concluded that, given the opportunity, Ed Fletcher III probably would have shot his own son.

The motion to reduce the sentence was thus respectfully denied. Before the sentencing, Judge Moon turned to Ed Fletcher III and asked, "Mr. Fletcher, this is your case. Do you wish to say anything on your behalf before I pronounce sentence?"

"No," Fletcher said.

Edward Fletcher III was sentenced to two consecutive sentences of life without parole in the Corcoran State Prison, about 50 miles south of Fresno.

On February 10, 1995, the judge in the civil case against the Fletchers ruled that Marjorie was not liable for the deaths of Walter and Carrlene Harper because she could not have foreseen that her husband would shoot them. "The fact that he was unpleasant when drunk or that he had threatened intruders or hunted animals is not sufficient to make homicide foreseeable. Mrs. Fletcher had no duty to warn or protect the Harpers under these circumstances." Grant Harper and Lisa Harper Henderson appealed the judgment.

On May 23, 1995, their lawyer informed the judge that Grant and Lisa had agreed to settle the case against Edward Fletcher III. "However," the lawyer wrote, "the Harpers' appeal of the summary judgment entered in favor of Marjorie Fletcher shall be preserved."

Marjorie Fletcher was living alone in Borrego Springs, where she received correspondence from lawyers and worried about money. "She was so far in debt that she talked about being a street lady," Audrey Hibdon said.

Although Hibdon, a native of San Diego with relatives in Fletcher Hills, knew that the Fletcher name meant land and money, she didn't see that kind of wealth in Ed and Marjorie's hands. Marjorie's parents had also been wealthy, but because they didn't like Ed — "they saw the abuse over the years," she said — and because Ed and Marjorie "drank up their money," Marjorie's mother arranged her estate so that all Marjorie received directly was the rent from her mother's house on Mt. Helix. "Everything else," she said, "was put into trust [for the three grandchildren]. And she would never, ever see it."

It was Marjorie's decision to remain in the house where the shootings had occurred. "Right after the murders, her son Eric took her to San Diego, and they put her into a recovery program, and after three days there, she was calling Eric day in and day out, several times a day, and telling him she wanted to come home," something no one in the family thought would be good for Marjorie. "They had called in a crew and cleaned up the house so that no one in the family, or I, when I went back, would have to see anything bad, but no one thought she needed to be there alone, but that's where she wanted to be, and finally Eric gave in, and his wife went and picked up Marge and brought her back to the desert, and this is where she stayed. She would drive into town and buy — finally, there weren't any businesses in town that would sell alcohol to her. Because she — it just got really bad."

During the year before the trial, Hibdon had driven Marjorie to the county jail once a week to visit her husband. "When he finally went to trial and was convicted and transferred," she said, "then she just didn't — there was no more desire to do anything. She didn't even want to leave the house."

By this time, Kent was also in prison. Her third son, who had been diagnosed as paranoid schizophrenic before the murders, was in a locked board-and-care facility. Eric, "the good son," lived on the other side of the county. One night at 11 o'clock, Marjorie fell while getting out of her car. She crawled into the house and pulled the phone off the nightstand to call Hibdon, who drove to the house. "I picked her up off of the floor and put her back on the bed — she was in screaming pain, and I said, 'Marjorie, let me call the doctor!'"

She said, "No, no, no, no, I'll be fine, I'll be fine, but you better come back early in the morning and feed the dogs."

Hibdon didn't want to leave, and later regretted it, but she left. The next morning, she went out to feed the dogs and found that Marjorie hadn't moved. She called the fire department and Marjorie was taken to Brawley Hospital, where she was found to have a broken hip. When she was released, Hibdon went to get her, and Marjorie came home. "She walked with a walker from then on."

Hibdon helped find homes for the three spaniels. "She would call and beg me to bring her some wine because vodka was making her violently ill. And I'd say, 'No, Marge, I can't do that. I just can't do that. I won't buy alcohol.'"

But Hibdon believes that Marjorie drank more and ate less. As May ended and the hot month of June began, "she would call me every single morning at seven o'clock and she would say, 'Oh, nobody's coming, and I haven't been doing much, and you don't need to come today,' and that's how it was the last ten days of her life. And so she probably didn't have a bite to eat, and just . . . nothing."

On that June morning, Audrey Hibdon received a call from Marjorie's cousins, who had come down to take Marjorie out to lunch. Marjorie's car was there, but no one answered the phone, and no one answered the door.

Hibdon said that she'd talked to Marjorie the day before at seven o'clock in the morning, the usual time. "Well, let me tell you where the spare key is," Hibdon told them, "and you can just go on in and see if she's all right, or would you rather I came out and did that?"

The cousins said they would much rather have the sheriff do

that. An hour later, the sheriff called Audrey Hibdon to say that Marjorie was dead.

When the funeral was held a week later, Hibdon didn't attend because she sided with her friend against what she saw as neglect. "To me, she was a black sheep that they wanted to forget about, and did."

There's no doubt another side to that story, or more likely many sides, all of them spinning like the mirrors on a whirling carousel, but Eric Fletcher would only agree to be interviewed if this story omitted all mention of his father and "where he is now."

"We want that to die," Eric said.

Carrlene Harper

At Eric's request, other family members declined to be interviewed, and Ed Jr. and his son Lawrence, who permitted one interview, deferred to Eric and canceled the second. You can hardly blame them for choosing silence, for wishing the name could mean one thing but not the other.

Each year, the UCSD alumni association awards the Carrlene Harper Memorial Scholarship to a fourth-year medical student who has gone above and beyond duty in his or her personal efforts to help others. In a color photograph taken beside a rippled lake, Carrlene Harper shields her eyes from the sun. In a photograph taken at Lisa Harper's wedding, Walter dances with his daughter. He's slim and dignified, about to waltz right out of view. He's wearing a tuxedo and a pink flower. He's as close to the camera as he was to the gun. It's impossible to imagine firing it. It's much easier to imagine the rage falling away, the gun lowered, Ed saying, "No, I must have lost my mind for a minute," and then telling people, years later, that from that moment on, he never drank again. "Another one of the experiences of life," as his grandfather would say, "where everything comes out all right."

Lisa Harper Henderson with her father, Walter Harper

THE TOOTHPICKS

A MEXICAN CARTEL IN SAN DIEGO

ONE

There's always a moment when it could have been prevented. You see it afterwards, when it's too late: that instant when the net fell and you caught him, only to let him go.

At 3:39 a.m. on January 7, 2007, the Little Italy district of San Diego was almost deserted, but Columbia Street had been plagued with car burglaries, so police officer Joel Schmid parked his patrol car and approached on foot when he noticed a pearl white Escalade stopped in the driveway of a condominium.

One door was slightly ajar, triggering the interior lights. Schmid could see shadows moving inside. He requested assistance from other officers and stepped quietly to the driver's-side door, where he confronted a Hispanic man in his thirties and two women, one of whom was sitting on the man's lap.

The man benignly handed Schmid a Mexican passport with what Schmid called a "real blurry photo." The name on the passport and on the U.S. visa tucked inside was Rubén Flores. A search of the Escalade produced a loaded Colt Mustang, seven cell phones, a blue

Viagra pill, the business card of a Chula Vista gun store, a permit for the American Shooting Center, and a folded sheet of white paper that resembled a faded receipt.

"On one side of the paper," Schmid testified, "was a kiss in lipstick, as if somebody with lipstick had kissed the paper itself and folded it up, and inside of that receipt, underneath the kiss, I found a crystalline controlled substance I believed to be methamphetamine."

The paper sealed with a kiss did, in fact, contain .07 grams of crystal meth, but that and the gun weren't enough to keep the man in the pearl Escalade for long. Five months later, he was busy in Chula Vista and Paradise Hills, executing plans that involved three assault rifles, six handguns, two Tasers, two duffel bags of Mexican and American police uniforms, five cars, a length of heavy chain, four padlocks, a blindfold, muriatic acid in quantities sufficient to dissolve grown men, and the belief that a rich Mexican family with businesses on both sides of the border would not call the FBI if a family member disappeared.

He was mistaken.

TWO

One Friday in May of 2007, a security camera mounted on a house in the gated neighborhood of Belmonte recorded a man in a polo shirt and jeans approaching the front door from a white Volkswagen Beetle. The man was thin and unremarkable except for the sharp point his receding hair made on his forehead and the equally sharp features of his face. He looked more Anglo than Hispanic.

He peered through the glass of the front door and walked away several times, waiting or looking for someone. After 12 minutes, he left a note on the front step.

The $1.5 million house he visited on Mansiones Lane belonged to 32-year-old Eduardo González Tostado, called Eddy by his cousin Sergio, and sometimes "Mandilón," which comes from the Spanish word for apron — el mandil — and means "whipped."

Eddy found the note when he returned with his wife Ivette and their six-year-old daughter from their regular weekend trip to Mexico, where he owned a house, a bar in Ensenada called El Blue Martini Lounge, and a restaurant in Tijuana called Mariscos del Pacífico. On the American side, Eddy owned a company that rented out trucks that carried goods from maquiladoras into the United States and two car dealerships in Chula Vista: Premiere I and Motorland Auto Sales.

Eddy's father-in-law was a neurologist in Tijuana, and Eddy, who had once been the starting quarterback on the only American-style football team in Ensenada, had earned a law degree from a Tijuana college called Centro de Estudios Superiores. He was famous in his hometown of Ensenada for being the first Mexican ever to win a 216-mile cross-country race through the Mexican desert called the Baja 250. Off-road cars like the one Eddy owned cost upward of $100,000, and year after year, the races were won by foreigners.

Eddy picked up the note on his front step. Urgent to call Robert it said in Spanish, and it listed a phone number. Eddy went to look at the surveillance video, and he paused the tape to show the man with the pointed hairline leaving his front door. He took some pictures of the screen. Then he drove to a nearby shopping mall and used a public phone — not his cell or house phone — to call the driver of the white Volkswagen.

According to Eddy, the conversation went like this.

"Is this Robert?" Eddy asked.

"Yes. Who is this?"

"You left me a note on my house," Eddy said.

The person calling himself Robert then told Eddy that he'd been sitting in a bar when he overheard some people planning to kidnap Eduardo González Tostado. These men in the bar had talked about where Eddy's businesses were and where his house was and what number you had to punch into the keypad at the gate to get to Eddy's house. For $30,000 (which was what, Robert said, those guys owed him), he would tell Eddy who these men were. For free, he told Eddy that the person who'd passed along the gate code was "El Arquitecto."

The architect was a friend of Eddy's named Eduardo Monroy, someone Eddy knew from vacations in Puerto Vallarta. Eddy had helped Monroy find an apartment and then had given Monroy work remodeling the patio at the Mansiones house, for which Eddy had given Monroy the gate code.

With this knowledge of a former friend plotting against him, Eddy drove back home, punched in the gate code that was now circulating among people who meant him harm, and went back to his wife and child. When his cousin Sergio arrived from Ensenada, Eddy showed him the note. Sergio would remember the note differently. Mandil, call me, Sergio recalled it saying, not Urgent to call Robert. In Sergio's memory, the note referred to Eddy by his nickname.

In any case, Sergio looked at the security video, studied the pale-skinned man with the pointed hairline, and told Eddy he'd once given that man a ride in La Jolla. The man in the video was the Tijuana boyfriend of someone Sergio knew, and his real name was Juan, not Robert.

So Eddy decided to look for the man in Tijuana. He took the photographs he'd made from the surveillance video across the border to his restaurant, Mariscos del Pacífico, and asked his staff if they'd ever seen this guy, Juan. Eddy told the manager to call him if the man in the video showed up.

Eddy also took the step of calling his lawyer to ask that he get a private investigator to find out who, exactly, Juan was and where he lived.

After that, Eddy and Juan spoke by telephone one more time. This time, Eddy told Juan that he knew his real name and did not intend to pay him anything.

Juan promptly lowered his informant fee to $6000.

Eddy still wanted to know if the kidnapping threat was serious, so he suggested that Juan meet him at Mariscos del Pacífico, but Juan refused, saying he didn't have papers and therefore couldn't go to Mexico, but he could meet Eddy at a shopping mall in the U.S.

Eddy didn't agree. They decided to talk again by telephone, but

Eddy never spoke to Juan again. The exchange did, however, initiate a crucial conversation between Eddy and his wife Ivette.

"I told her if I ever were kidnapped, go to FBI," Eddy said.

PHOTO COURTESY OF LA-CH.COM

Kidnap victim Eddy Tostado

THREE

At about this time, two things happened. A For Rent sign went up in front of a plain brown house in a tight cul-de-sac at 1539 Point Dume Court in Chula Vista. Fifteen-year-old Derek and his friend Freddy watched from their garages as the house that had been occupied by a family with a teenaged daughter was visited first by prospective renters and then by the new tenants, who were not a family but a pair of guys. They were Hispanic, in their twenties or early thirties, Derek guessed, and they spent an awful lot of time driving to and from the house. One guy in particular would drive to the house, carry in some grocery or duffel bags, then get back in his red MR2 and drive away. A couple of hours later, he'd be back and do the same thing. A lot of cars, in fact, rolled in and out of Point Dume now: a black 2008 Escalade with newly purchased rims (not stock, Derek noticed), a silver Ranger, a gray Corolla, the red MR2, and a black Lincoln truck.

Meanwhile, an old friend of Eddy's got in touch to apologize. Three years earlier, Eddy Tostado and his friend David Valencia had sometimes gone out to clubs with Monroy (the architect), and their respective wives and girlfriends. One night the women were dancing for Eddy, David, and the architect, and David started punching and kicking his girlfriend. When Eddy tried to stop David, David grabbed a bottle of whiskey and hit Eddy on the head with it.

Eddy nearly passed out, blood gushing from an inch-long cut. The architect tried to calm David down, as Eddy remembered it, but security took David out, and Eddy went to his father-in-law's clinic to have the gash on his head swabbed and sealed with butterfly bandages.

David Valencia

That was the last time Eddy saw David Valencia until May of 2007, when Juan showed up on Eddy's front step with his kidnapping story, and David Valencia started telling Eddy's car detailer (who came to Eddy's house every Friday) how sorry he was about hitting Eddy with that whiskey bottle and how much he wanted to talk to Eddy and make it right. The car detailer even tried to use his own phone to call David so that apologies could be made and friendship restored. They didn't reconcile, though, until Eddy heard that his former friend David had been in the hospital. Okay, Eddy decided, and he called.

David and Eddy met at a coffee shop, where David said he was sober now, living in the U.S. with his wife and family. David's son was playing soccer, his daughter was riding horses — he was doing family things now — and maybe Eddy's daughter would like to come ride horses sometime. By the time Eddy and David parted that day, Eddy had promised to buy some cars for David at an upcoming auction, just like he used to do.

FOUR

On Thursday, June 7, Eddy Tostado and David Valencia went to a car auction. David picked out a car and a pickup truck and left. Eddy, because he was the one with the dealer's license, bid on the cars David wanted, among others, and at around 7:00 that evening met David in a Starbucks in Chula Vista. David was waiting on the patio outside, which was really just two green umbrellas on the sidewalk, hemmed in by the bug-spattered bumpers of trucks. Southwestern College sits across the street, so students flow in and out all day, buying lattes and frappés.

Eddy and David chatted about when and where the cars would be ready, and Eddy had pushed his chair back to go when David said, "Wait, let me buy you a coffee."

Eddy said he didn't want any coffee. It was too late at night, he said, and coffee would keep him awake, but David insisted, so Eddy relented, and as he sat there on the strip mall sidewalk, the temperature, which had been 63 degrees, dropped ever so slightly, and the cloudy sky pinkened, as it does even in the gloomiest month of the San Diego year, and another person who was not who she said she was walked into the picture.

"Nancy," David called her. She was young and thin and pretty and Latina, like lots of girls who go in and out of that Starbucks, but she dressed expensively, decked out in Louis Vuitton. She was about five feet six and very fit, Eddy noticed, as if she worked out. She had short hair and what Eddy called a "little nose."

Nancy Michelle Mendoza Moreno

No sooner had Nancy left their table to buy something inside Starbucks than David, the reformed family man, began asking Eddy — the man kidded for being under the thumb of his wife — what he thought of this Nancy girl. Did Eddy like her? David pulled out his phone to show Eddy a few pictures of his girlfriend, who was Nancy's friend. David happened to have a few shots of Nancy too, posing in a bikini.

Eddy admitted she was nice-looking. He thought or didn't think about his wife. He thought or didn't think about the child his wife was expecting, the lateness of the hour, the coffee in his hand. After Nancy of the little nose bought whatever it was that she wanted from Starbucks and talked briefly in Spanish to the two men at the table, David assured Eddy that Nancy and her friends were okay. Eddy could go out with Nancy if he wanted, and there would be no *problema* whatsoever.

Unfortunately, Eddy Tostado believed this. He'd been a football quarterback and a Baja racing champion and maybe he could still turn a girl's head. He believed — and who hasn't believed a flattering lie? — that when Nancy called David a few seconds later and asked to speak to Eddy, she was very interested in him, so interested that she wanted Eddy to write down her phone number. Eddy took it down. He had that phone number with him the next afternoon, Friday, June 8, when he was sitting with his good friend Carlos — his daughter's godfather — at the Butcher Shop Steakhouse. He decided to call up Nancy and ask if she wanted to have dinner with him.

Nancy said *Sí*. But she didn't want to have dinner at the Butcher Shop. She suggested they take a little trip across the border to the Cantina de los Remedios, where there would be mariachis and margaritas.

Nancy told Eddy she had to pick up her passport before they could go to the cantina. She wanted to change her clothes too, so she told Eddy to meet her at the Starbucks in Sunbowl and follow her to her aunt's house in Chula Vista. He did this. He drove his black Range Rover to yet another Starbucks and began to follow Nancy's silver Jeep Liberty with Mexican plates and a Hank Rhon bumper sticker. He followed as she turned right, left, right, left, right in a maze of streets named for promontories: Point La Jolla Drive to Morro Point to West Point to Barrow to Dume. As Eddy Tostado sat in his Oxford leather seats outside a house far shabbier than the one in which his wife and daughter lived, he received a call from some employees at his dealership, Premiere I, who complained they hadn't eaten lunch yet even though it was now past 6:30, and they needed some money from him. He was going to have to drive over there and give them some cash.

Nancy said that was okay. She'd just run in and change while Eddy took care of those guys. In fact, maybe he should stop at the liquor store for some Buchanan's Red Seal whiskey. Her aunt wasn't home, she said. Eddy could come in, and they could have a drink before they went to Tijuana.

So Eddy drove to his dealership, then to Bobar Liquor, where he bought whiskey, cognac, and condoms, and back into the maze again, to 1539 Point Dume Court, which Derek and Freddy could have told him had recently been rented by a couple of Hispanic guys, not anyone's aunt.

1539 Point Dume Court

It was now past 7:00 and cloudy, just like the day before. A gloomy twilight hung over the roof and the evergreen pear tree. In the pop-out window where other neighbors with the same house plan displayed porcelain angels, swans, flowers, and small American flags, there hung a bent venetian blind. Eddy noticed that Nancy's car, which had been parked in the driveway outside the garage door, was now gone. He watched a blue Chevrolet SUV roll slowly into the cul-de-sac, turn a tight circle around the evergreen pear, and leave. The driver of the car was a man wearing a hat. Uncertain, Eddy called Nancy to ask if she was expecting someone, such as a boyfriend. "No," she said. She wasn't. "Come on in."

He walked to the front door of the house where Nancy waited

for him, and when she opened the door, he noticed she had not yet changed her clothes.

Before Nancy had even closed the door they tackled him.

At first there were two men. He felt one grabbing his feet and another grabbing his back. Two men dressed in police vests and hats, their faces covered with ski masks, ran toward him. They were carrying rifles. Eddy tried to shake off the two men who were tackling him, and they began to hit him. One of the masked policemen hit Eddy on the bridge of his nose with the back of a rifle. Then they hit him with the rifle in the back and on the legs. He heard and felt the stun gun after that. With each shock delivered to his spine and the soft tissue of his lower back he heard *dak, dak, dak, dak*. Ten times in less than a minute.

Eddy started to shake, and he fell facedown on the floor. Everything that had been in his bowels and bladder came out. He was nearly unconscious, and he couldn't move to get away. They went on hitting and kicking him. On the back of his head, he felt a single hard blow. They handcuffed him behind his back. They taped his ankles together. They put a towel over his head. All he could see were the shoes of the men walking around him and the guns lying on the floor — two handguns and one rifle.

In Spanish, they said, "You're not so tough anymore."

"Look at you now," they said.

"You stink."

They left him like that for a few minutes, mocking him for the stink he made, and then they wrapped him with a towel and dragged him to the back of the house, where they blindfolded him and stopped to take roll. Eddy heard them count to seven in Spanish. Seven against one. They didn't say anything else to him, but they took Eddy's Rolex and went off to another room. He could hear their voices but not the words.

Then one voice in particular, the one he would come to know well, told Eddy, "You know what this is. We want money from you, and you're not going until you pay us."

For a few minutes more, they left him in his soiled clothes on the carpet. Then two of them dragged Eddy to the bathroom and warned him that if he tried to escape or look at their faces they would kill him. Eddy was allowed to use one hand to strip off his underwear, rub at the filth with a wad of toilet paper, and put the same jeans back on. Then they snapped his handcuffs shut and took him to a closet, where they wrapped a chain around his legs. They threaded the chain through the handrail of the stairs nearby, weaving the links noisily in and out of the iron pickets, a memorable sound to a person wearing a blindfold.

This was his place now: a three-by-five-foot closet in which he could not stand up, a wad of blankets and sheets, an uncased pillow, his dirty pants.

"Call me Jefe Uno," a voice told him. Boss Number One.

"Call me Jefe Dos," another said. Boss Two. The third man was Jefe Tres, and the others didn't get to be *jefes* at all.

This is when they began to describe their credentials. Boss One told Eddy they'd done this before. They were professionals. Before Eddy, they'd gotten the brother of El Pareja, someone named Junior or Junior Gordo, Balitas, and Quilino. Eddy knew who El Pareja was — a guy from Tijuana who'd been arrested a year or two back. The brother of El Pareja, they told Eddy, had not behaved. They killed him. Balitas, on the other hand, got the money real fast and in only a day was free again. A million dollars, Balitas had paid.

Boss Three told Eddy — and this made all the jefes laugh — that Nancy had done the same thing to Quilino that she did to Eddy. She lured Quilino right to the jefes. Quilino had not been as fast as Balitas, though, and he had to stay for a whole month before his family paid enough to get him free.

Boss One wanted Eddy to know, if it wasn't clear enough already, that they were up here from Mexico doing whatever they wanted. He told Eddy he had the balls to do it right here in the United States, where he'd moved after those guys in Tijuana killed his brother. "I saw you at the races in Laughlin," Boss One told Eddy.

Boss One even told Eddy who his dead brother was. His brother was Palillo — Little Stick, or Toothpick. Eddy knew the name. Six or eight years before, Eddy had seen Palillo racing motorcycles in Baja. They had a mutual friend from high school.

What did it matter if he was blindfolded? He'd seen Nancy. He'd seen David Valencia. And now he knew quite a bit about Boss One. Surely this meant they would have to kill him.

"Give us a million," Boss Two told Eddy as he sat in his soiled jeans, unable to touch or examine the open sores on his back made by the Taser shocks. "Give us a million and you can go the next day like Balitas."

Eddy said he didn't have a million. "Maybe $100,000," Eddy told them, "$200,000."

"No, no," Boss One said. "You can do better than that."

They left him inside the closet and went to have some drinks in another room. Later, they put a sleeping pill in his mouth.

FIVE

On the first morning of his imprisonment, Eddy awoke to the sound of a sliding-glass door, then water splashing in the backyard. A voice asked if he needed something. He said he needed to go to the bathroom, so they brought him a bucket.

The guy in charge of the bucket had a Cuban accent, and the Cuban said his name was Asere. The other two who weren't jefes also told Eddy their names. Morro was just a kid, and Tío had middle-aged hands. Tío told Eddy, "If you want something, let us know and I will cook whatever you need."

So there was the bucket and the chain and the closet with the wad of sheets, the bruise on his nose where the rifle butt had struck him, and there was the weird kindness of food cooked to order. In the background, day and night, the TV was on, tuned to the Copa Oro, soccer's gold cup. The night before, when they were shocking and beating him and tying him up, Mexico was beating Cuba 2–1.

Tío told Eddy, "Don't do anything stupid, and you won't be killed."

It was three or four hours before the jefes showed up. Boss One told Eddy it was time to call his wife and ask for money.

Eddy and his family used phones that function more like walkie-talkies than regular phones — push-to-talk phones, as they're known, offer a cheaper way to talk across the border. Boss One searched Eddy's phone for the list of contacts, found Eddy's wife, and pushed the button.

Somewhere far from the closet, in a place where the closet could not even be imagined, Ivette's phone started beeping. She was in the car with her daughter and her sister, and she was in no mood to take a call from a husband who hadn't come home the night before.

Boss One held Eddy's phone near his blindfolded face, and Eddy heard his daughter, not his wife, say, "Hey, Papi, where are you?"

Eddy didn't answer that. "How are you, darling?" Eddy said. "What are you doing?"

She said they were driving in the car.

"Hey, I want to speak with Mami," Eddy said. "Can you put her on the phone?"

"No, she doesn't want to talk to you because you got drunk and you went — you didn't come to sleep in the house." When his daughter held the button down, Eddy could hear his wife refusing to talk.

Eddy's daughter handed the phone to her mother anyway, and Ivette took it — or at least it sounded as if she did — but she didn't say anything to Eddy.

Boss One pushed the button and Eddy tried to talk. "I have problems," he said. "I need you to hear me good because I'm trying to—"

"No," Ivette said. "You have no problems. You just went and had some beers and you didn't come home."

Then his wife hung up.

Boss One and Two were incredulous. "What?" they told Eddy. "Don't you have the balls to tell her to shut up and listen?" They laughed.

Eddy sat with his legs shackled. His blindfold cut into the sore on his bashed nose while Boss One pushed the button to call Ivette again.

"If you do or say something stupid," he told Eddy's blindfold, "I will kill you." This time Boss One held the phone to his own face.

"*¿Tu querer?*" Ivette said, thinking it was once again her husband on the line. What do you want?

"Hey, stupid bitch," said a voice she hadn't heard before. "If you want to see your husband again, you have to listen. You want me to send him in pieces by mail to your house?"

At first she was silent. She came from a city where this happens, where angry people who are never found or punished deliver bodies in Igloo coolers with handwritten diatribes on the outside, a city where headless bodies are left in the dirt near elementary schools and the disembodied heads are wrapped in duct tape.

"No, no, no," she said. "What do you want?"

Boss One held the phone to Eddy's blindfolded face. Eddy could see a little bit down his nose: shoes, hands, the cuffs of pants.

"Hey, round up some money," Eddy told his wife. "Try to sell the house. Call my uncle. He has the papers for the house in Tijuana. Try to sell the bar." He told her whom to call — her mother, her father, her grandmother. See if they would help. He told her to sell all the cars at the dealership, the motorcycle, and the race car. "Sell the restaurant." Everything.

"Yes," she said. "I'll do whatever you want."

On the same day, Eddy told Boss One it would be better for him to negotiate in the future with his cousin, not with Ivette, who was pregnant. That was when Eddy gave his cousin an alias that was also a clue. "Talk to my cousin 'Brenan,'" Eddy told Boss One.

There was only one person who called Eddy's cousin Sergio that: Eduardo Monroy, the architect, the former friend who'd given out Eddy's gate code to kidnappers. Monroy liked that kind of joke. Monroy called Eddy "Mandilón" because he thought that was funny, and he called Sergio "Brenan" after a Mexican talk show host who, like Sergio, dressed up all the time. Eddy was hoping that Sergio would somehow make the connection.

Boss One agreed to negotiate with Brenan. When Boss One added Eddy's cousin to his own cell phone directory, that's how he listed him: BRENAN. He didn't know that his conversations with Eddy's cousin would all, from this point on, be listened to and recorded either by the FBI or by Ivette and Sergio, who used little pocket tape recorders they were told to carry everywhere they went. Boss One had, after all, kidnapped Balitas and Junior Gordo and El Pareja's brother and Quilino, and he didn't expect Ivette to disobey him when he said not to call the police.

But Ivette remembered what Eddy said when they got the first hint that someone was after him. "Call the FBI," he told her, and that's exactly what she did.

SIX

According to the FBI, many kidnappings investigated in San Diego involve Hispanic residents who have ties to Tijuana or Ensenada. Some of the family members who report abductions say, "We were hesitant to come, but there've been three kidnappings in our neighborhood alone, and they never got their family members back, so we're coming to you for this one." By "neighborhood," the FBI agent said, the callers really meant their circle of friends.

Sometimes the abduction is discovered because the police find a body, track down the family, and are told, "Yes, there were ransom calls, but we didn't call the police."

In Paradise Hills, above a flat, barren park, a green slope rises steeply to the 6500 block of Garber Street. The houses on Garber Street have been there a long time, and they're showing their age, but they mostly have the pitched roofs and boxy shape of houses in a child's picture book. In the rooms of one of these houses, two men have long ago been strangled, and their bodies have been taken south to San Ysidro, where the barrels full of acid are heated by propane not far from the shuffling hooves and sweet grassy smells of horses.

SEVEN

ays and nights passed inside the house at Point Dume to the televised shouts of the Copa Oro. The house held almost nothing but a TV, mattress, duffel bags of police uniforms, and three containers of muriatic acid such as you might have if you were keeping down bacteria levels in your pool, though the house on Point Dume had no swimming pool. By adjusting his blindfold, Eddy made enough of a gap that he could see Tío's Timberland boots, Morro's Air Jordans, and Boss One's Prada shoes. He could see Boss One's Cartier watch and guess ages by the skin on their hands. Boss One was young and thin. Boss Two was young and thin. In time, he saw Tío had a goatee and was in his 40s.

They told Eddy to keep his mouth shut and stay over there because they didn't know if he was gonna make it or not. They compared him unfavorably to another hostage, Jorge, who was an old man but was always calm and did push-ups. Jorge, they kept for 28 days.

When Eddy broke down, they said what was he, a girl?

"I'm a — I'm a human being," he said. He said he missed his daughter and he missed his family, and he wasn't going to go with other women anymore. He wasn't going to be like that again.

They said, nah, men needed girls on the side, but Eddy said, "No, no, no. No more," in Spanish. *Nunca jamás.*

Asere was the one who stayed all night at Point Dume, so he talked more than the others. "The last time they pay me, like, $5000," Asere told Eddy, "but I was coming and going. This time I'm gonna only stay here because I want to get more money."

He told Eddy about coming to the U.S. on a boat from Cuba, about how his wife and daughters were still there.

EIGHT

On Sunday, June 10, the FBI recorded and translated a conversation among Eddy, his wife, and Sergio. As Eddy spoke, Boss One was listening. As Ivette spoke from a room in her sister's house, a device she couldn't see was transmitting her voice to agents she'd been warned by Boss One not to contact. She had moved out of the Mansiones house and her daughter was staying with relatives, but she was afraid that somehow the kidnappers were watching or listening to her too.

Eddy asked Ivette how she was doing, and she tried to answer.

"I'm fine, sweetie," she said in Spanish. "I'm hanging in because these people are going to let you out alive. I want you back alive, and I'm going to do everything possible — everything — to come up with everything they want because I know that, that, that, that they're going to respect you and, and, and, and, you know, I want you back alive, alive and in one piece, I want you alive. I love you."

"Yes, honey," Eddy told her while Boss One listened and watched. "I love you very much. Uh, do it, do…make sure…be smart about what you're going to do and, uh, try and figure out what you can do about the house."

It wasn't a good time to be selling a house. A six-month wait, Sergio told Eddy. That's what the real estate agent predicted.

Eddy listed again all the things Ivette should sell: the race car, motorcycles, every car on the lot at Premiere I and Motorland. Talk to "our buddies," he told her. "Maybe they can do us a favor there. Talk to, to your girlfriend and everything, tell her, uh, her dad, and we'll see what happens. Let's see if he can help us out."

She said she would.

In the living room on Point Dume Court, the TV was tuned to Univision, and Honduras beat Mexico 2–1.

NINE

Monday, Tuesday, Wednesday, Thursday, and Friday, Eddy wore the same dirty clothes and the same blindfold. He had been allowed to keep one possession: a photograph of his daughter. He slept in the closet, and Morro, the young one with very short hair and Air Jordans, said this wasn't a good job but his girlfriend was pregnant. Mexico beat Panama in the Copa Oro. The money was not coming together the way Boss One expected. Sergio and Ivette had put the Mansiones house on the market at a low price, completely furnished, for a quick sale, but it hadn't sold, and they had come up with only a fraction of a million so far, most of it from a relative who had agreed to purchase Eddy's mother's house in Ensenada for $150,000.

TEN

In the movies, ransom money always looks so clean and powerful. Bricks of hundred-dollar bills lined up like paper bullion.

On Friday, June 15, FBI agents drove with a SWAT escort to the Premiere I car lot owned by Eddy Tostado to pick up the ransom money gathered by Ivette and Sergio. Then the agents drove back to the FBI office on Aero Drive.

The money was in a Georgia-Pacific paper box, not a briefcase: $193,900 in used, wrinkled $20 bills that Ivette and Sergio had gathered and counted and subdivided into stacks of $2000 within stacks of $10,000 using the kind of multicolored rubber bands you find at the back of the junk drawer in your kitchen.

The four agents faced with $193,900 in this form had a problem: they couldn't possibly write down almost 10,000 serial numbers. The ransom drop was too soon.

Instead, they took pictures of the front bill and the back bill of each $2000 stack, photographed each $50 and $100 bill, and those became the "bait bills," the ones they could identify later. Then they put all the money back in the box and drove with the

SWAT escort back to Premiere I cars and returned the money to Ivette.

"The plan after that," the agent in charge testified, "was to get with our technicians to secure a ransom bag." That way, "We would be able to surveil the drop with the money because there would be a tracking device in the bag."

ELEVEN

At 10:29 that night, Boss One called Sergio (whom he knew by Eddy's code name Brenan) to talk over the terms of a ransom drop.

"What's up, Brenan?" Boss One said, speaking in Spanish except when he used the word okay. "Hey…I was thinking, man. Look, I don't have problems with your friend…with your cousin, man. Okay? I have problems with those fuckers out there. You know who. Those who think they're killers. Okay? You must know. Look…I don't have any problems, man. Let's make… Do you want to go ahead and make a deal or what? So we can work it out tomorrow?"

"Yes, well, I really do," Sergio said. "We just want him to be okay."

The deal was that Sergio would give Boss One the nearly $200,000 he had so far, and Sergio would keep trying to sell Eddy's race car for another $100,000, and Boss One, because he was such a nice guy, would drop the total ransom from $2 million to $700,000.

"I'm asking if you want to make a deal, man. Tomorrow," Boss One repeated. "Because I don't have problems with him, man."

"I don't have problems with him" is something Boss One said several times to Sergio, as if this were a very critical distinction: the impersonal kidnapping versus the personal one, the thing you do for money versus the thing you do out of hatred or revenge.

"If it were up to me," Boss One went on, "I'm— I'm very comfortable over here, man. The guy is there. If it were up to me, he can stay there for months, okay? But I'm not an asshole, and I don't have problems with him, man. It's— it's just that they brought him to me. And the people that he was with — you know who he hangs around with, man, with those fuckers from out there — he's working with them, and I have problems with them. We're at war, man. I think you must have heard, right?"

In his rambling, Boss One changed arguments ever so slightly, from "I don't have problems with him" to "I have problems with the people he's with." It's personal but it's indirect. The associates of Eddy Tostado are on the other side of what Boss One calls a "war," the logic goes, and they must be punished, so Eddy's going to pay.

Sergio didn't seem to know what Boss One was talking about. Sergio and Eddy grew up together in Ensenada, and then Sergio went into the army for seven years. When Sergio came back, Eddy had a lot more money than he used to have, which was kind of suspicious, but on the other hand he had married the daughter of a neurologist.

"No," Sergio told Boss One, "I really don't know what the problem is, but — uh — but that's fine. That's fine. Yes, we just want him to be okay, you know. We're his family, you know, and…we want the guy to be okay."

Boss One didn't explain what he meant by a war, or which guys Eddy Tostado was supposedly hanging around with. Instead, he became more conciliatory — conspiratorial, even. The deal Boss One was offering to Sergio had to be a secret from those other ones, the shadows that were making all this unpleasantness happen, the ones that had brought Eddy to Boss One in the first place.

"Okay," Boss One said. "Well, try hard so you won't worry so much about it, man. I'll leave it at seven for you, man. What do you think? At seven. Go ahead and tell his wife right now, man. Look, tomorrow I'm going to call you during the day, man. I'm going to call you during the day tomorrow…no — uh — and I'm going to ask you, 'So what's up? Do you have those? How much do you have?' And you tell me, 'The two hundred.' Okay? I'm going to do you the favor, and you're going to listen to what I'm telling you, man. Okay? Don't talk too much. I mean, listen to what I'm telling you. Because if you talk too much, man, he's going to stay there for months, man. People are leeches, you know. I'm the good guy over here, man, and I'm going to let him go, just like that fucking young man left. But he's not going to leave like that, in payments, man. You know what I mean? You give me those two hundred tomorrow, and if you have the other hundred — when you have them, man. You know what I mean? On Sunday, I mean, I'm not in a rush, man. You know what I mean? You call me, you tell me, and we'll work it out. People come to an understanding when they talk things over. You know what I mean? And so that — so that we can see something and believe you…and you just try hard and get the rest together. What do you think?"

Sergio heard this speech late at night after a week spent trying to sell things to people who knew it was a desperation sale and so offered the lowest possible price. When he wasn't trying to sell things for more than people wanted to pay, he was trying to calm down Eddy's pregnant wife, who could hardly talk without crying, she was so terrified, and he'd been staying in the United States every night and carrying a tape recorder with him everywhere he went and talking to federal agents of a country not his own.

I'm going to do you the favor.

I'm the good guy here.

Don't talk too much.

If you talk too much, he's going to stay there for months.

We're at war, man. You must have heard.

"No," Sergio said, and then, because it was kind of hard to know what the question was, he said, "Well, yes, that's very good, that's very good. Just, uh, well — just keep putting him on so that we can talk to him. But, uh, we, yes, we want him to be okay, and, uh, we're going to try to…to get it all together soon, as much as we can."

Boss One kept talking in that scary, circular way.

"Don't think that it's just me," Boss One said. "There are a lot of us, you know, and people, well, they — they have delusions that your buddy has money. I know how things are. I know what is going on with those guys. They're treating him well because I tell them to. Okay? I want— when I call you tomorrow I'm going to ask you, 'Hey, man, how's it going? How much?' "

The conspiracy thing again. The importance of keeping Boss One's deal a secret while somehow appeasing the shadow men, the ones with delusions about how much money Sergio should be coughing up.

"Later on at night around this time," Boss One continued, "I'm going to call you to see if you got the hundred, man, or if not, then on Sunday when they give it to you. Right after that, you're going to keep scraping around, man, so you can gather the seven. And if you don't gather them, call me. We'll call each other and we'll come to an understanding, man. You know what I mean? Like I said, I'm not an asshole. My word is good, man. Uh, and then at night, if you have the other hundred, the one that you're trying to get, you put them in a little bag with the jewelry that this guy says he is going to give to a friend of mine — to me, and you're going to talk to him, man."

Talk to whom? To Eddy? To Boss One's friend? At least Sergio knew what jewelry Boss One was talking about. While Eddy was passing the hours in his closet, thinking and thinking and thinking about who had done this to him and how he could possibly get himself free, he'd hit upon the fondness his kidnappers had for expensive watches. That was, after all, one of the first things the jefes did after they tackled and shocked Eddy — they stole his Rolex. And by peeking underneath his blindfold, Eddy had seen Boss One's Cartier watch. "I have more watches," Eddy told Boss One and

Boss Two. "Six more," each one worth between $6,000 and $10,000. Ivette had already gathered these watches up as an offering.

"I want this guy to go home, man," Boss One went on in his crazy way. "And to keep working, man, because the guy is a worker and we're going to work. Okay? There's no problem, man. And I don't have any problems with him. I know that he's not a killer or anything, man. But those guys did it to me with, with — the guys who bring work to your cousin, and, well, I have problems with those guys, man. Well, you already know, man. That's another issue."

There it is again: Boss One thinks Eddy is just a worker, not a killer, but those who bring work to Eddy are people Boss One hates.

"Tell me that you already sold everything," the Boss told Sergio. "Tell me, 'You know what, man? We're screwed. I gathered — I'm selling everything. We're screwed. I already sold jewelry and everything. Here are the two hundred, give me a chance.' "

These are Sergio's lines, the script he's supposed to follow, and Boss One says that his own lines, when prompted by Sergio, will be, "Okay, man, give me that. My people are going to go pick it up."

Sergio listened.

"And that's it," Boss One said. "I'm going to call you at night to see if you got the hundred, and you're going to put them separately with the jewelry. I'm going to do you the favor, man. You know what I mean? I'm going to do this favor, you…and your…this guy… Eduardo."

"Okay," Sergio said. "Got it. Thank you." The signing off seemed to take forever, to be as uncertain as the life of the man Boss One called "this guy Eduardo."

"All right, then," Boss One repeated. "I'll give you a call early tomorrow, man."

"All right. Got it."

"All right then. You understood me, didn't you, man?"

"Yes, I understood you. Okay. Got it."

"All right, man. I'll call you tomorrow."

"All right," Sergio said again. "Thank you."

No sooner was Sergio free than the phone beeped again. It was Boss One. "Oh, I was going to ask you, man, uh…are you going to deliver the papers or…?" *Papeles*, Boss One said. In Spanish, "paper" is slang for "money."

"Yes, yes, yes," Sergio said. "Just the way you told me… tomorrow."

TWELVE

The FBI's plan was to do a controlled ransom drop. They would watch it happen and go "wherever it led us."

Up to a point. The FBI has no authorization in Mexico, so if Boss One picked up the $193,900 and drove south on I-5 until he came to San Ysidro and the signs that say "Last U.S. Exit" and kept going, Ivette had a choice. Did she want the agents to pull over Boss One's car and arrest him, even though no one knew where Eddy was? Or did she want to let the money cross over that line and disappear, maintaining the trust of the kidnappers who might still, in the future, lead them to her husband?

Ivette decided not to risk Eddy's life. If the car went over the border, she said, let it go.

THIRTEEN

aturday, June 16, was the eighth day that Eddy Tostado woke up in the same clothes. It was the eighth day that someone brought him a bucket to use as a toilet. But that afternoon, Asere and Morro let him come out of the closet, go into the living room, and listen, blindfolded and handcuffed, to the Copa Oro. At 1:00 p.m., Canada was scheduled to play Guatemala, and at 4:00, the U.S. would face Panama.

There's a Popeyes Chicken and Biscuits half a mile from the FBI office, a suitably obscure place for Ivette and Sergio to drive with a box full of money. Three agents met them in the back parking lot while other agents waited at the FBI building, and the SWAT team prepared its gear, and two pilots waited on the runway of Montgomery Field, all of them together weaving a large invisible net.

It was two o'clock in the afternoon, moist and warm. The usual clouds had burned off, intensifying the scent of fried chicken. Diners sat outside under striped red-and-yellow umbrellas and knew nothing. Ivette's role was to stay in the parking lot and wait, while Sergio's was to drive his red Dodge Ram truck wherever Boss

One told him to drive.

An agent fitted Sergio with a body wire, a device like a pager that attached to his belt. Wires circled him beneath his clothes. There was a small microphone.

Ivette was frantic and distraught. Sergio was scared but trying not to look it. The agents transferred "bricks" — bundles of wrinkled $20 bills — from the Georgia-Pacific box to a briefcase provided by the FBI. The surveillance units would be listening, an agent told Sergio. She told him to keep his conversations to a minimum — talk only to the kidnappers — and then she gave him a phrase to use in the event that he felt something bad was happening. He was supposed to say, "Don't shoot."

Popeyes restaurant at 3489 Santo Road, where the FBI prepared Eddy's cousin to make a ransom drop to kidnappers.

As soon as all the money was in the briefcase, Sergio's phone beeped. It was 2:20 p.m.

"Go," the agent told Sergio, and he went.

The recording made using Sergio's body wire is 53 minutes long. It's mostly silence and the exterior swish of cars as he drove, and although the FBI was supposed to be able to hear the whole thing live, something failed. A recording was made, but no transmission went out. Sergio was completely and totally alone, though he didn't know it at the time.

"I'm on my way, man," Sergio told Boss One. "The thing is, I had to drop off the lady here" — meaning Ivette — "because she was with me, you know. I'm on my way over there, all right? I have everything with me."

"All right," Boss One said. "Just make sure no one follows you, all right, man? Do things right. Listen to what I tell you, man, okay? Don't let anyone follow you or anything."

"No, don't worry," Sergio said. "We want this guy to be fine. Don't think that."

"All right, then. Uh, where are you? Which— what street? Are you still at Lowe's or what?"

Sergio said where he was, and Boss One began to give him directions. Take 805 south. Exit Plaza Boulevard. Wait at the Thrifty gas station.

From the gas station, someone appeared to begin following him.

Take 54 west. Exit National City Boulevard.

The FBI had already photographed the Rolex watches from every possible angle because Ivette had been afraid to find a jeweler to open them up and write down the serial numbers. These and the $100,000 Sergio had yet to get were the assurance that the kidnappers would want Sergio to go on living. He was not bringing the watches today, just the money.

Sergio drove down the ramp from Highway 54 into National City, then turned right into the drive-in movie theater that became, twice a week, a popular swap meet. Guaranteed Vehicles – Yes, the sign said. Discount Prices – Yes.

Boss One asked Sergio if he saw the broken tree and the fence with the gap in it. Sergio did. Boss One told Sergio to drive up to that broken tree and park his truck and leave the door open and walk into the swap meet through the gap in the fence and go inside the bathroom and not look back until they called him.

Sergio did all this without knowing that the wire had failed. The recorder on his body was collecting every sound he made, but no one was listening as he stepped out of his truck. No sniper in an unmarked car could actually hear him right then if he shouted, "Don't shoot!"

The asphalt at the swap meet is bumpy. The old humps where cars would park on a slight rise for a better view of the drive-in movie screen still curve in half moons like crop circles. Rusty poles that held speakers stand pointlessly askew. Huge potholes crater the ground, and the ancient trailers of the Keystone Trailer Park stick up over the ragged chain-link fence just high enough to make you feel observed. Sergio walked over the asphalt humps to the white cinder-block bathrooms. He did not look back.

Before he even entered the bathrooms, Boss One called Sergio and told him he could go back to his truck, and when Sergio stood once more before the open door, the briefcase and all the money were gone. The first ransom had been paid.

"Does my cousin need any clothes?" Sergio asked Boss One.

"No," Boss One told him.

There was nothing else for Sergio to do but call the FBI, say it was done. It was only then, at 2:50 p.m., that the agent in charge realized that the reason she had not heard anything for the last 30 minutes was the wire had gone down and they had not surveilled the ransom drop.

She got on the radio and told everyone the last known location — the swap meet. She told the ten agents in the surveillance unit (eight of them in separate cars, two in a plane), the sixteen members of the SWAT unit, and her own squad of three others to go to the swap meet, turn their radios to the frequency of the "beacon" transmitter that was inside the ransom briefcase, fan out, and listen.

Thirty people now began to search.

FOURTEEN

A half hour later, at 3:20 p.m., one of those agents waited in his car near 28 Las Flores Drive, a Chula Vista house rented to Jorge Rojas López and identified as "pertaining to the subjects of the case." There in the driveway was a gold Mitsubishi Lancer with Baja plates. He made a note of that. He parked a short distance away and adjusted his rearview mirror to show anyone coming or going from that house. He thought, mistakenly, that the briefcase held a tracking device, not a beacon. That was the original plan. (A tracking device sends out data to a computer, which would show the location of the device on a GPS map, but a beacon transmits an audio signal.)

As it became clear that he should be listening for a beacon, the agent turned his radio to the right channel. He heard a beep. Thirty seconds passed before he heard it again. Then, as the signal became stronger and more regular, a gold Mitsubishi Lancer driven by a lone Hispanic male approached and passed his car.

He let it turn the corner, and then he began to follow it, simultaneously calling for the plane to come to his location. Soon the Lancer had an entourage, which followed it first to a Comfort

Inn in National City, where it stopped for ten minutes, and then to the Tropical Oasis All Natural Juice Bar on Telegraph Canyon Road. Somewhere in this time period, $180,000 disappeared.

Click. A photograph was made at 4:38 p.m. Two young Hispanic men in white shirts — not just the one who drove the car from Las Flores Drive — left the juice bar and got back in the Lancer.

It could not have seemed good that the Lancer headed south. And still farther south. Straight down I-5 toward Mexico.

The kidnappers who picked up the ransom spent $400
at Neiman Marcus Last Call in the Las Americas mall.

But then the Lancer took the very last exit. The men who had picked up the ransom were going shopping at the Las Americas mall, from which you can see, but not touch, Mexico. More precisely, they were going to Neiman Marcus Last Call, which has a very extensive video security system. Every dull, ordinary thing the men did — every shirt held up to the light, every sole examined in the shoe department, every smile exchanged with the young female clerk — was recorded. For a few very odd minutes, a woman left her toddler asleep in a stroller near a man who was buying clothes for a hostage.

They spent nearly $400 in cash.

Outside in the parking lot, agents who had followed waited in their cars. A single-engine Cessna droned overhead. Everyone noted the time in surveillance logs: at 4:50 p.m., the two men who'd been photographed at the juice bar came out of the mall with shopping bags.

Their destination was 1539 Point Dume Court.

FIFTEEN

These are the things that happened in the next two hours.

Sergio and Ivette went to the house on Mansiones Lane. They were still trying to sell it and gather more money.

Agents began to park near the house at Point Dume.

Eddy Tostado was allowed, for the first time in eight days, to shower. Boss One and Boss Two gave him the designer clothes they'd picked out at Neiman Marcus Last Call: shoes, socks, boxers, Chip and Pepper jeans (too long), and a $90 dress shirt (too tight across the chest). This gave him hope. Of course, it was a mediated hope. Boss One told Eddy he was going to get a break. He was going to let Eddy go free while Eddy tried to sell his house. "But," Boss One also told him, "we know where your mother lives and we'll kill them all" if Eddy didn't pay up.

Eddy Tostado was then allowed to make what's called a "proof-of-life" call. Sergio and Ivette were relieved and happy. Eddy was buoyant. "My love," Eddy called his wife. "Te quiero," he said. I love you. He said there was no price he could put on being with her and his daughter again.

At 6:17 p.m., the gold Mitsubishi Lancer left Point Dume Court.

At 6:29 p.m., the red MR2 that Derek and Freddy had seen so many times also left Point Dume Court.

Corner of Brandywine and Olympic Parkway in Chula Vista

At the intersection of Brandywine and Olympic Parkway, two separate groups of three SWAT team cars were waiting with rifles and noise grenades that are called "flash bangs" because they make an explosive noise when detonated but don't throw off shrapnel. As people in cars on their way to movies and restaurants and gas stations and their own houses waited for the light to change, a flash bang was thrown onto the hood of a gold Mitsubishi Lancer. A flash bang was thrown onto the hood of the MR2. Traffic stopped. The man who stepped out of the MR2 was five feet six and weighed approximately 140 pounds. He had a goatee and hands that Eddy had seen from beneath his blindfold. His name was Raúl Rojas Gámez, otherwise known as Tío. Among the $6963.52 in cash that he carried were four $20 bait bills. All four serial numbers matched those written down by the FBI.

When the driver of the Lancer was ordered to step out of the car with his hands up, turn around, and face away from the officers, he instead lay facedown on Olympic Parkway.

"Get up," the agents shouted at him.

But Jorge Rojas López stayed, as the agent put it, "proned out on the ground."

He stayed there like that for two to five minutes, as agents ordered the passenger of the Lancer to exit the vehicle and walk slowly toward them. The passenger was Juan Francisco Estrada González, whose voice Eddy would soon identify as Boss Two's.

Inside the Lancer, agents found the receipt for Eddy's new clothes, the brown leather briefcase Sergio took to the swap meet, a shoebox from Neiman Marcus Last Call, and two cell phones containing, among other contact numbers, one for someone identified as BRENAN who had the same phone number as Sergio. That phone also contained the number provided to police by David Valencia during an arrest earlier in 2007, one for Juan Laureano Arvizu (the man videotaped leaving a note at Eddy Tostado's house), and, under the letters MANDI, the gate code needed to enter Eddy's neighborhood.

From Rojas himself, police seized $3206 in cash and found another bait bill. In his pocket was the key to the pearl white Escalade he'd been sitting in when arrested five months earlier. In the Las Flores house a few hours later, agents would find, among other evidence, four handguns and a photograph of Rojas with people presumed to be his wife and children.

SIXTEEN

Back on Point Dume, residents who tried to go home were stopped outside the cul-de-sac. Besides all the SWAT cars, neighbors could see Chula Vista police cars and news vans. Fifteen-year-old Derek, who was already home at the time, tried to run out onto the lawn to watch. A SWAT agent pointed a rifle at him and ordered him back into the house. He complied, of course, but he held his father's cell phone to an upstairs window and took the photograph that would appear first on his MySpace page and then as an exhibit in the trial.

In Spanish and English, an FBI agent spoke into a PA system. All over Point Dume, in the houses and yards, you could hear her voice repeating, "This is the FBI. We have you surrounded. Please come out of the house with your hands up."

SWAT agents holding submachine guns and body bunkers — bulletproof shields — moved in pairs toward the house. When no one responded to the agent's amplified voice, a designated team approached the front door with a "breacher," or police battering ram. They had just reached the door with it when the first SWAT agent in line shouted that the handle of the door was turning.

In the next moment, Eddy Tostado stepped out into the intoxicating summer twilight and was saved.

SEVENTEEN

He was saved, but he was also interrogated. In the police station later that night, at five minutes to midnight, one detective and two FBI agents, including the one who helped Ivette and Sergio prepare the ransom money, asked Eddy to identify himself and describe his ordeal. He told them, in halting English, about Monroy and Nancy and the stun gun and the bucket that was his toilet and the chain and the rifles, the Copa Oro, the Cuban, Boss One, and Boss Two.

"Did you ever think of escaping?" asked the detective.

"Yes."

"Did you try?"

"No."

"Why do you think they came after you?" the detective wanted to know.

"Because I'm from Ensenada," Eddy said. "That I have money from Mexico. I know, I know, from Mexico," he stammered, and the transcriber of the tape wrote that the rest of what he said was unintelligible, or "(UI)." Many things in the conversation were "(UI)."

"(UI) We know," the detective said. "We've done a lot of checking and stuff, and why do you think specifically [that] afternoon?"

"Because the uh, the other guy told me and uh, uh, (UI) we never found out (UI) my— my (UI) people are friends…"

"Um-hmm."

"They're a nice and they do their own thing. But I know people from— from one of them (UI)."

"We know that too," said the detective.

"I'm a (UI)."

"You're, like, independent?"

"(UI) know them."

Mumbling can be a sign, obviously, of evasion. It can also be a sign of someone talking too softly in his second language well after midnight directly following a harrowing SWAT team rescue and eight days of imprisonment in a closet.

"So let me just — let me just be honest," the detective said. "You have friends and possibly some family in Arellanos?"

A member of the Arellano Félix cartel of Tijuana killed López's brother, Palillo.

"No, no family."

"No family? Just friends?"

"Yeah. No family."

"No family whatsoever."

"None whatsoever."

"How do you know those people?"

"(UI) from the, uh, places." From Ensenada, Eddy said. A shop associated with off-road race cars.

I don't have problems with him, man, Boss One told Sergio the night before the ransom drop. *It's— it's just that they brought him to me. And the people that he was with — you know who he hangs around with, man, with those fuckers from out there — he's working with them, and I have problems with them.*

The detective wanted to know if Eddy's captors knew that Eddy was friends with "those guys."

Eddy said he thought so. He told the detective that Boss One (Rojas) said his brother Palillo got killed by those guys.

Eventually, the detective said, "You know we got these guys, right?" referring, this time, not to the cartel but to Boss One, Boss Two, Tío, Morro, and Asere, the five men who had been arrested leaving the Point Dume house.

"Yeah," Eddy said.

"And you know they're gonna come to court…and they're gonna say, 'Well, this guy, you're the bad guy.' What are they gonna say about you?"

"I don't care," Eddy said, all three words perfectly intelligible.

The conversation was not over. The detective would ask if Eddy ever told Rojas he could get money from the Arellanos.

"No," Eddy said.

"Why didn't he kill you?" the detective asked.

"Was waiting, I think maybe, for the money and then after kill me," Eddy said.

After that, Eddy was shown a group of photographs and he identified the man who left a note at his house: Juan Laureano Arvizu. He listened to recordings and correctly identified the voices of Boss One and Boss Two. He said things that made sense and things that didn't make much sense. It got later and later — the interview continued until 2:00 a.m. Finally, toward the very end, Eduardo González Tostado said something clear. He said he was reborn.

EIGHTEEN

The trial took place nearly a year and a half later, in October and November of 2008. Jorge Rojas López, Boss One, and Juan Francisco Estrada González, Boss Two, were charged with kidnapping for ransom and bodily harm. Eddy Tostado testified, and the defense attorneys for Rojas and Estrada did exactly what the detective told Eddy they would do. They said Eddy was the bad guy. They said that "one of the superiors at the top of this organization" — the Arellano Félix cartel — "goes by the moniker of El Mandil" and that workers of the cartel have told Mexican authorities that El Mandil had been heard on two-way radios giving all kinds of orders, including kidnapping orders.

"And guess who the authorities believe that El Mandil is — the Mexican authorities? The Mexican authorities believe that El Mandil is none other than Eduardo González Tostado."

Defense attorneys were given permission to cross-examine Tostado in an order dated October 21, 2008, and signed by Judge Charles Rogers that states:

1. Witnesses have told the FBI and the Government of Mexico

that Mr. Eduardo González Tostado uses the nickname "El Mandil."

2. Credible evidence exists that Mr. Eduardo González Tostado is a prominent member of the Arellano Felix Organization (AFO).

3. The AFO is a criminal organization involved in drug trafficking, money laundering, kidnapping, and murders.

But an order signed by Judge Rogers on September 3, 2008, creates a different impression about the witnesses and the evidence against Tostado. "With respect to the material itself [information the prosecution team had regarding possible criminal activities of Eduardo and Sergio Tostado], the court discovered no material that was based on personal knowledge and not based on hearsay regarding Mr. Eduardo Gonzalez Tostado and Mr. Sergio Tostado. None of the material consisted of eyewitness or first-hand information of the participation by either of them in the AFO or any of its activities or in criminal activities in general."

None of the material consisted of eyewitness or first-hand information. It was all hearsay. In Mexico, that hearsay resulted in an arrest warrant. Eduardo González Tostado was wanted there in September of 2008 for organized crime. During the trial, as a consequence, jurors heard FBI testimony about the Arellano Félix cartel, and they also heard what Jorge Rojas López said to Sergio when he didn't know he was being recorded: "I don't have any problems with him." Although Rojas repeatedly vowed to take revenge on the Arellano Félix cartel, he said he didn't have any problems with Eddy.

Eddy testified that Rojas checked Eddy's reputation in Mexico after Eddy became a hostage. "They like done some investigation during the week," Eddy said, "and let me know that I won't have any problems."

"Who told you that they had done investigations on you?"

"Boss Number One."

"Did he tell you what type of investigations had been done?"

"Yes. Ask some people from Ensenada also that they knew and that I knew, and they asked the word around Mexico and find out."

"Find out what?"

"That I just work and have my business, that's how I make a living, and that I didn't have nothing to do with his brother."

NINETEEN

When the trial ended on November 21, 2008, Jorge Rojas López and Juan Francisco Estrada González were convicted of kidnap for ransom with bodily harm and sentenced to life without parole. Rojas is considered the leader of a gang named Los Palillos—the Toothpicks--in honor of his murdered brother, and the gang has 17 members, including the five who were arrested that night at Point Dume. What follows is an account of their various fates.

In March of 2013, Rojas went on trial again for the kidnapping, torture, and murder of Teódulo Espinoza Andrade, Jaime Gómez Coronado, Guadalupe Becerra Herrera, Francisco Olguín Verdugo, Ricardo Escobar Luna, Mario Baylón García Jr., Ivan Lozano Váldez (aka Junior), César Uribe, and Marc Anthony Leon Jr. — nine killings in all — making him eligible for the death penalty. Rojas is further charged with robbery, attempted robbery, attempted kidnapping, shooting at an inhabited house, and attempting to murder a peace officer. After hearing eight months of testimony, the jury began deliberating on October 27, 2013, and had not reached a verdict when this book went to press in 2014.

Raúl Rojas Gámez, or Tío, pled guilty to kidnapping.

The men Eddy knew as Morro (Carlos Peña García) and the Cuban Asere (José Olivera Beritan) were indicted in the kidnapping of Tostado, as was David Valencia, the man who introduced Eddy to Nancy.

In 2012, José Olivera and David Valencia were tried and convicted again, this time for the kidnapping and murder of César Uribe and Marc Anthony Leon Jr. In the trial, Uribe was described as Valencia's best friend and a former associate in drug trafficking. On May 3, 2007, David Valencia lured Uribe and Leon to the ranch in San Ysidro where he kept the horses his daughter liked to ride, the same horses, perhaps, that Valencia told Eddy Tostado his own daughter ought to come down and ride some time. At the ranch, Uribe and Leon were kidnapped. They were taken to the house on Garber Street and held while Uribe's family made two ransom payments totaling several hundred thousand dollars. The second ransom payment was supposed to set them free, but Uribe and Leon were strangled and their bodies were taken back to Valencia's ranch and placed in barrels of acid heated by propane. Two years later, bones, teeth, and body parts were found in vats of brownish gelatin. Both Olivera and Valencia are serving multiple life sentences without possibility of parole.

Juan Laureano Arvizu, the man who left the note on the Tostados' doorstep, is still wanted by the FBI, which describes him as an avid gambler who likes to bet on professional sporting events and go to nightclubs. A Mexican national with no legal American papers, Laureano, or "Chaquetin," is charged with robbery, attempted kidnapping, shooting at an inhabited house, attempted murder of a peace officer, the kidnapping and murder of Ricardo Escobar Luna, Mario Baylón García Jr., Ivan Lozano Váldez (aka Junior), César Uribe, and Marc Anthony Leon Jr.

Eduardo Monroy, the architect who gave out Eddy's gate code, is still at large.

Ernesto Ayón, a Los Palillos member charged with kidnapping, killing, and dissolving César Uribe and Marc Anthony Leon Jr. in muriatic acid, is also at large.

Nancy Mendoza Moreno was paid $15,000 for her role in luring Eddy Tostado to the house where he was held for eight days. She disappeared after his rescue and wasn't found for three years. In 2010, U.S. officials found her working in a Tijuana law office. She was arrested, extradited, and tried for her role in the kidnapping of three men, including Eddy and 25-year-old Balitas or "Little Bullets," the man Eddy heard about the first night of his imprisonment: *Balitas got the money real fast and in only a day was free again. A million dollars, Balitas had paid.*

In the summer of 2012, when Nancy was 24, she was acquitted of charges that she told Los Palillos where to find Balitas, but convicted of bringing Eddy Tostado to the house on Point Dume Court and of helping them to kidnap Jorge García Vazquez at a traffic stop. García was shot with a Taser, held for 22 days, and released after his family paid approximately $500,000. (Eddy also heard that story presented as a warning: Quilino was not as fast as Balitas, and he had to stay for a whole month before his family paid enough to get him free.)

Nancy Mendoza Moreno was sentenced to life in prison without possibility of parole on August 23, 2013.

As for Eddy Tostado, he closed his Tijuana restaurant, Mariscos del Pacífico, in October of 2008. When asked during the trial why he closed it, he said a waiter and a bartender had been shot and killed there and that two barrels of acid found to contain human remains had been left outside. Federal police in Mexico subsequently arrested an alleged drug trafficker, kidnapper, and extortionist known as "El Teo." Teodoro García Simental was known for disposing of his enemies in gruesome ways, especially for beheading them and dissolving bodies in acid. They also arrested an employee of his known as "El

Pozolero," or the stew-maker, who admitted to dissolving at least 300 bodies.

Eddy Tostado continues to be appreciative of his rescue and to cooperate with the prosecutions of Los Palillos "even though there have been attempts on his life and the lives of family members," according to Mark Amador, lead prosecutor. Amador further stated that Mr. Tostado has not been charged with any crimes in the U.S. relating to alleged cartel activities or drug trafficking. "At the time of the first trial, there was an arrest warrant in Mexico but no arrest warrant in the United States. Since that time, the Mexican arrest warrant has been rescinded by the Mexican government. Our understanding from Mr. Tostado and his attorney is that the arrest warrant was quashed by legitimate legal means, using what's known in Mexico as the amparo process. Therefore, to our knowledge, there are no charges pending against Mr. Tostado in the United States or Mexico."

When asked if other cartel associates like Jorge Rojas López continue to cross the border and dare, as Rojas bragged, to bring cartel methods to the U.S., Amador said there were similar kidnapping crews that remained active after the takedown of Los Palillos in 2007. "These groups band together in criminal conspiracies to rob, kidnap, extort, and kill."

In light of these continuing threats, Mark Amador's statement to the jury during his closing arguments still rings true. Amador asked the jury to consider the massive pile of evidence against Boss One and Boss Two — the photographs, the video surveillance, the cell phones, the bait bills, the receipts, the recorded phone conversations — and say, "We know you did this. Doesn't matter who you picked out."

From a public safety standpoint, it truly doesn't matter whether Eddy was an innocent victim or a guilty one. If he had not been saved and had not testified, a man with ID that says he's Rubén Flores could be driving through your neighborhood right now with a friend. They have a nice car and nice watches. They know where to buy pool-cleaning supplies, and they own a large collection of guns. They're pulling into the driveway of a rental house with an attached garage, and when they knock, they are welcomed into its empty rooms. They open the back door and walk casually into a well-fenced backyard where, as it happens, there is no pool. They say they'll take it. They pay cash.

THE TOOTHPICKS: LOS PALILLOS GANG MEMBERS WHO ARE STILL AT LARGE

Juan Laureano Arvizu. Charged with leaving a warning note on the Tostados' doorstep. At large and wanted for five murders, kidnapping, and robbery. Avid gambler.

Eduardo Monroy. "The Architect." Charged with giving Tostado's gate code to co-conspirators.

ACKNOWLEDGMENTS

The author gratefully acknowledges the support of Jim Holman, Judith Moore, and Tom McNeal, without whom these stories could not have been written, and the tireless editorial assistance of Heather Goodwillie, whose gift is to question every word and assumption.

ABOUT THE AUTHOR

Laura Rhoton McNeal holds an MA in fiction writing from Syracuse University and is the author, with her husband Tom, of four young adult novels published by Knopf: *Crooked* (winner of the California Book Award in Juvenile Literature), *Zipped* (winner of the Pen Center USA Literary Award in Children's Literature), *Crushed*, and *The Decoding of Lana Morris*. Laura's solo debut novel, *Dark Water*, was a finalist for the National Book Award and the winner of the San Diego Book Award in young people's literature in 2010.

SAN DIEGO READER BOOKS

The San Diego *Reader* archives contain more than 40 years of unique journalism, and it's our mission to reintroduce the best of our writing to a new generation of readers in book form, free from advertising. San Diego *Reader* Books are available from a variety of popular online stores including *Amazon.com, BarnesandNoble.com, Apple.com* and *KoboBooks.com.*

JOIN OUR MAILING LIST

Be the first to find out about new releases and special offers like free copies of our eBooks. Visit *www.sdreaderbooks.com* to sign-up and to see a complete list of current and forthcoming books.

www.ingramcontent.com/pod-product-compliance
Lightning Source LLC
Chambersburg PA
CBHW051723040426
42447CB00008B/952